Mission

The *Community Literacy Journal* is an interdisciplinary journal that publishes both scholarly work that contributes to theories, methodologies, and research agendas and work by literacy workers, practitioners, and community literacy program staff. We are especially committed to presenting work done in collaboration between academics and community members, organizers, activists, teachers, and artists.

We understand "community literacy" as including multiple domains for literacy work extending beyond mainstream educational and work institutions. It can be found in programs devoted to adult education, early childhood education, reading initiatives, or work with marginalized populations. It can also be found in more informal, ad hoc projects, including creative writing, graffiti art, protest songwriting, and social media campaigns.

For us, literacy is defined as the realm where attention is paid not just to content or to knowledge but to the symbolic means by which it is represented and used. Thus, literacy refers not just to letters and to text but to other multimodal, technological, and embodied representations, as well. Community literacy is interdisciplinary and intersectional in nature, drawing from rhetoric and composition, communication, literacy studies, English studies, gender studies, race and ethnic studies, environmental studies, critical theory, linguistics, cultural studies, education, and more.

Subscriptions

Donations to the CLJ in any amount can be made with a check made out to "Coalition for Community Writing" with *Community Literacy Journal* in the memo line.

Send to:

Veronica House
University Writing Program
Anderson Academic Commons – 282
2150 East Evans Ave
University of Denver
Denver, CO, 80210

Donors at the $40 level or above will receive a courtesy print subscription of the academic year's issues.

Cover Artist and Art

"Beauteous Chaos" by Michael Lone Wolf Orrell

Michael Lone Wolf Orrell is an Irish, Cherokee, and Jewish hybrid who lived most of his life in Amory, Mississippi. He's a humanitarian who does not condone violent behavior against the vulnerable. You can find more of his work in *Mississippi Prison Writing* (VOX Press) and *Juke Joint* Issue18. Michael is presently an ABE Language Arts Writing Tutor, Literacy Math Tutor, and an Assistant Tutor in Social Studies at

Unit 30 in Parchman State Penitentiary, Mississippi. Michael had no expectations of the future nor any visions or dreams. He wasn't seeking to find them, but they sought and found him.

Artist's statement: I was sitting at the table on the zone. I began to do an inventory of myself. I saw all these things in my life that appeared to be beautiful to my conscious ego. But my subconscious ego showed me "how" I have been living. My subconscious "who" I am let me see the beauteous chaos in my life. Although there is colorful beauty, there are also sharp edges

Submissions

Submissions for the Articles section of the journal should clearly demonstrate engagement with community literacy scholarship, particularly scholarship previously published in the *Community Literacy Journal*. The editors seek work that pushes the field forward in exciting and perhaps unexpected ways. Case studies, qualitative and/or quantitative research, conceptual articles, etc., ranging from 25-30 manuscript pages, are welcome. If deemed appropriate, we will send the manuscript out to readers for blind review. You can expect a report in approximately 12 weeks.

Community Literacy Journal is committed to inclusive citation practices and encourages authors to cite and acknowledge ideas of BIPOC scholars, activists, and organizers in community literacy.

The *Community Literacy Journal* also welcomes shorter manuscripts (10-15 pages) for three sections reviewed in-house:

Community Literacy Project and Program Profiles will discuss innovative and impactful community-based projects and programs that are grounded in best practices. We encourage community-based practitioners and non-profit staff to submit for this section. Profiles should draw on community literacy scholarship, but they are not expected to have the extended lit reviews that are customary in the articles section of the journal. If you are a community member wanting to submit, and it is your first time writing for an academic journal, we are happy to offer mentorship and answer questions. Pieces co-authored by multiple stakeholders in a project are also welcome.

Please submit using our online submission system. Contact the Project and Program Profiles Editor, Vincent Portillo, with questions at portilvi@bc.edu.

Issues in Community Literacy will offer targeted analysis, reflection, and/or complication of ongoing challenges associated with the work of community literacy. Potential subjects for this section include (but are not limited to): building/sustaining infrastructure, navigating institutional constraints, pursuing community literacy in graduate school, working with vulnerable populations, building ethical relationships, realizing reciprocity, and negotiating conflicts among partners. We imagine this as a space for practitioners to raise critical issues or offer a response to an issue raised in a previous volume of the *CLJ*.

We encourage community-based practitioners and non-profit staff to submit for this section. If you are a community member wanting to submit, and it is your first time writing for an academic journal, we are happy to offer mentorship and answer questions. Pieces co-authored by multiple stakeholders in a project are also welcome.

Please submit using our online submission system. Contact the Issues in Community Literacy Editor, Michelle LaFrance with questions at mlafran2@gmu.edu.

Coda: Community Writing and Creative Work welcomes submissions of poetry, creative nonfiction, short stories, and multi-genre work on any topics that have ensued from community writing projects. This may be work about community writing projects, and this may be expressed in ways we have yet to imagine. We ask authors to include a personal reflection about the submission itself--information about your community writing group (if you belong to one); your personal journey as a writer; what inspired you to write your piece; and anything else you'd care to share about your life--as an invitation for the author and Coda's readers to consider writing and activism as intertwined. Contact Coda Editors with questions at Coda.Editors@gmail.com.

Authors interested in reviewing for the CLJ should contact Book and New Media Review Editor Jessica Shumake at jessica.shumake@gmail.com.

Advertising

Community Literacy Journal welcomes advertising. The journal is published twice annually, in the Fall and Spring (November and June). Deadlines for advertising are two months prior to publication

Ad Sizes and Pricing

Half page (trim size 5.5 x 4.25): $200
Full page (trim size 5.5 x 8.5): $350
Inside back cover (trim size 5.5 x 8.5): $500
Inside front cover (trim size 5.5 x 8.5): $600

Format

We accept .PDF, .JPG, .TIF or .EPS. All advertising images should be camera-ready and have a resolution of 300 dpi. For more information, please contact the journal co-editors at editorsclj@gmail.com

ISSN 1555-9734

Community Literacy Journal is a member of the Council of Editors of Learned Journals.

Production and distribution managed by Parlor Press.

Publication of the *Community Literacy Journal is made possible through the generous support of the University Writing Program at the University of Denver. The CLJ is a journal of the Coalition for Community Writing. Current issues and archives are available open access at https://digitalcommons.fiu.edu/communityliteracy/*

Editorial Board

COMMUNITY LITERACY journal

COMMUNITY LITERACY journal

Fall 2023
Volume 18, Issue 1

1 *Guest Editors' Introduction*
Gabrielle Isabel Kelenyi, Chad Seader, Alison Turner, Ada Vilageliu-Diaz

Articles

3 *African Americans in Ghana: Enacting Literate Acts of Healing from Epistemic and Ontological Harm*
Mohammed Sakip Iddrisu

24 *Saliendo del Pueblo: Migration, Literacy, and Non-Literacy Practices in a Mixtec Farmworking Community*
Guadalupe Remigio Ortega

42 *Finding the Lorde in Me: Using Lordean Counterstory to Thwart Bureaucratic Violence in Community-Based Literacy Projects*
Teigha VanHester

Issues in Community Literacy

57 *Radically Imagining Community Programs: Reflection, Collaboration, and Organizer Toolkits*
Erin Green

Book and New Media Reviews

72 *From the Book and New Media Review Editor's Desk*
Jessica Shumake, Editor

73 *Unsettling Archival Research: Engaging Critical, Communal, and Digital Archives*
Reviewed by Michael Harker

80 *Searching for Literacy: The Social and Intellectual Origins of Literacy Studies*
Reviewed by Jamie D. I. Duncan

Coda

90 *Editors' Introduction*

93 *First Pride Parade in My City*
Saurabh Anand

95 *Three Poems*
Mara Lee Grayson

102 *Institutional Departure*
Sarah Puett

113 *Gratitude*
Tracey Bullington

118 *"Pros & Cons Panel Presentation 2023, Call for Presenters"*
Evan Harris

121 *A Meta-Staging of the Initial Investigative Operatics Working Group, With [x number of] Original Cast Members Playing All the Parts.*
Bethany Ides, Fan Wu, Ora Ferdman, and Zoe Tuck

136 *Against Forgetting: Quilt Pieces and Reflection*
Susan Naomi Bernstein

Guest Editors' Introduction

Gabrielle Isabel Kelenyi, Chad Seader,
Alison Turner, Ada Vilageliu-Diaz

For this special issue of *Community Literacy Journal*, we invited submissions from practitioners who are applying methods and practices as a means for "imagining a world that doesn't exist" (Ozy Aloziem). The call for papers developed from a discussion initially shaped by Coalition for Community Writing Emerging Scholars, who were inspired by the 2023 Conference on Community Writing's theme: radical imagination. Conversations over several months highlighted this special issue as an opportunity to intentionally feature new voices and BIPOC perspectives. As guest editors for this special issue, we are proud to publish research that reflects ideas, values, and possibilities that deepen these foundational discussions.

As emerging editors navigating the business of academic publishing, we're familiar with the rhetorical and systematic frictions shaping our work in community writing. It often seems as if the values and practices needed to support truly transformative antiracist, decolonial, anticapitalist community potentials are at odds with the conditions of our employment and the necessities to simply get by in the US. For us, this tension between the possibilities we strive to manifest and currents of the neoliberal university is a source of both frustration and creative resilience. While working with the authors featured in this issue, we felt a sense of comradery seeing them wrestle with the same questions and challenges that we face in our own practices. As drafts circulated back and forth between editors and authors, we offered each other fresh perspectives that inspired new ideas and strategies to strengthen our respective communities. The issue reflects the knowledge-sharing and mutual support that lies at the heart of our work to continuously reimagine what community writing and literacy can do despite institutional and structural limitations.

First, in two peer-reviewed articles, authors focus on how culturally specific rhetorics operate to heal and (dis)empower communities, respectively. In **"African Americans in Ghana: Enacting Literate Acts of Healing from Epistemic and Ontological Harm,"** Mohammed Sakip Iddrisu explores the ritual of African Americans visiting the Ancestral Slave River Park in the Central Region of Ghana. Iddrisu frames this site as a "space where African Americans and other Africans in the diaspora symbolically inscribe their names as evidence of their return to their ancestral homeland," a "gesture" that he argues is "in defiance of colonial structures." Traveling to this site, Iddrisu asserts, is a "radical literate social act" that heals ontological harm, manifesting in literacy practices ranging from embodied rituals of bathing, writing on the Memorial Wall of Return, dress, and naming.

While Iddrisu's piece highlights the textual and non-textual literacies of African Americans in Ghana, Guadalupe Remigio Ortega radically reimagines literacy and non-literacy in **"Saliendo del Pueblo: Literacy and Non-Literacy Practices in**

a Mixtec Farmworking Community." By highlighting her parents' deliberate choices to prioritize orality, human connection, stories, spirituality, and connection to land to communicate both within and without their Mixtec farmworking communities, Remigio Ortega aims to transform "non-literacy into a positive, intentional, and proud choice, an act of self-preservation and resistance" for Latinx Indigenous folx. Her parents' stories demonstrate how literacy and non-literacy interact, bringing questions about who and how literacy empowers and disempowers to the fore.

Then, rooted in her own experience as a first-year professor at a private, predominantly-white university, Teigha VanHester's piece **"Finding the Lorde in Me"** draws upon Audre Lorde's work on eros and anger to expand Aja Martinez's concept of counterstory and develop strategies BIPOC scholars might use to navigate institutional violence. VanHester's concept of *Lordean counterstory* deviates from Martinez's model via its focus on embodiment. By honing in on our emotions and understanding how those emotions relate to the systems we're positioned within, VanHester claims that Lordean counterstory has potential to build community and fight against the forces of neoliberalism by opening new possibilities.

Finally, Erin Green's **"Radically Imagining Community Programs: Reflection, Collaboration, and Organizer Toolkits"** addresses the challenges of developing community writing projects through a discussion of their own public-facing syllabus project and organizer toolkits for social justice. Green's piece argues for the importance of flexibility and adaptability when designing and implementing community writing projects despite scholars' "ambitious" goals because "community literacy work is challenging and often comes with unforeseen disruptions." This Issues piece serves as a useful reminder for community writing practitioners that we should move beyond the idea of reciprocity and focus instead on "more emergent strategies for enacting radical change."

Taken together, these pieces show that imagining a better future isn't enough; rather, radical imagination requires that we engage one another, experiment, and play outside predetermined structures as a means of guiding structural change and embodying new ways of being in the world. In the words of Michael Lone Wolf Orrell, the creator of this issue's cover art, these new ways of being require "sharp edges" to arrive at "colorful beauty."

We are pleased to also include two book reviews, edited by Jessica Shumake, and the fourth publication of "Coda: Community Writing and Creative Work," edited by Kefaya Diab, Chad Seader, Alison Turner, and Stephanie Wade.

Articles

African Americans in Ghana: Enacting Literate Acts of Healing from Epistemic and Ontological Harm

Mohammed Sakip Iddrisu

Abstract

Black scholars across disciplines including literacy studies have theorized literacy practices and traditions that people of African descent employ towards healing. In response to Black rhetorical scholars' call for the discipline to examine Black diasporans' healing practices in charged sites of trauma such as the Pikworo Slave Camp in Ghana, I devise methods, informed by Indigenous decolonial approaches, to study and theorize African Americans' creative literacy practices of healing at a historic site in Ghana.

Keywords: Healing, Literacy Practices, Indigenous Decolonial Methods, Sankofa, Ontological Harm, Epistemic Harm

Introduction

Ours is a time of intense racial reckoning and communal investment in diverse healing practices that span across local, national, and transnational borders. In these times, many communities such as the African diaspora—specifically African Americans—are reimagining and investing in creative literacy practices of healing, as decolonial endeavors, from the harms of colonialism and anti-Black racism. These healing practices have found expressions in various cultural spaces in post-independent Ghana, West Africa, a transnational rhetorical site beyond the Euro-American context of the U.S. which is deeply and systematically anti-Black and inherently colonial.

Historically, Ghana has been a cultural site of refuge and anti-colonial protest for African Americans especially since the U.S. Civil Rights Movement in the 1960s. Given its colonial history as a former British colony and one of the first Black African nations to gain independence from colonial rule, the nation-state of Ghana, as an institution, has had a long history of beckoning African Americans to return "home." Such institutional calls have historically created expectations of how African Americans should *be* in Ghana and have scaffolded many of the projects—symbolic and material—that African Americans have initiated and participated in in Ghana. For a start, consider the fact that in 1957, at the behest of the nation-state, Martin Luther King Jr. and other prominent African Americans traveled to Ghana to participate in the new nation's independence celebration, a symbolic yet impactful voyage that shaped King's civil rights rhetoric upon his return to the U.S. (Gaines). In the contemporary, the nation-state continues to call African Americans to Ghana. This call is motivated by the nation-state's own structural and economic interests to attract capital investment (Attiah). Thousands of African Americans have responded to this call (Dini-Osman; Taylor) especially since 2019 when the government of Ghana initiated the "Year of Return" to commemorate 400 years (1619-2019) since the first enslaved Black Africans were violently captured and shipped from the coast of West Africa to present day Virginia, stripping them of their very humanity. What I investigate here are their practices of healing, particularly those that circumvent the institutional status quo and primary economic interests of the nation-state. Participants in my study creatively initiate literate social practices geared towards reclamation of their humanity and healing from the ongoing residues of colonialism and contemporary anti-Black violence.

For centuries, African Americans have been engaged in different types of healing traditions manifested through spirituals, healing narratives, healing circles, wounded healing, and diasporan literacy (Boutte; Hill; King). In addition to these healing traditions, several Black scholars including John Henrik Clarke and bell hooks argue that people of African descent need to engage in heritage knowledge—African Americans' knowledge and memory of their collective histories—to heal and attain "complete self-actualization" (hooks 47). In Clarke's view, heritage knowledge, which includes re-establishing some ties with Africa, will liberate Black communities "from the old ties of bondage" (86). Against the backdrop of over 400 years since the African Holocaust, brutal murder, exploitation of African labor, and denial of access to their ancestral homeland and cultures, African Americans are returning to African countries including Ghana to reconnect with their ancestral heritage as a way of healing and reclaiming their humanity. Indeed, Black scholars argue that the African Holocaust or the Holocaust of Enslavement caused varied degrees of emotional, physical, and psychological trauma and wounds from which Africans and people of African descent need to heal (Browdy and Milu 235; Karenga).

As a Black African from Ghana, I recognize the atrocious impact that slavery and colonialism has had and continue to have on Africans and people of African descent. Accordingly, I share in the call for healing among continental Africans and Africans in the diaspora. My positionality and experiences of living in Ghana as an *African* and in the United States as a *Black African* deeply inform my approach, particularly my methods and analyses, in this study. As an insider (African) and outsider (not African American), I approach this topic with a personal and nuanced understanding of the historical, cultural, and communal intricacies involved. My own complex identities and positionality allow me to explore this topic with profound sensitivity and empathy and a sense of shared cultural heritage with my African American participants.

In this study, I explore African Americans' literate social practices of healing in Ghana and theorize how they initiate creative literacies shaped by Indigenous epistemologies. My study focuses on participants engaging in practices aimed at reclaiming their humanity and healing from the ongoing impacts of colonialism and contemporary anti-Black violence. My analyses are predicated on the fact that in a world where anti-Black racism runs rampant, healing has become a desirable and prioritized goal of every Black person. Rhetorical scholars Ronisha Browdy and Esther Milu contend that "Black people everywhere, continental and Diasporic, must seek approaches to healing from the physical and psychological wounds caused by the African Holocaust" (235). The prolonged experiences of colonialism, slavery, anti-Black racism, and ongoing coloniality have resulted in Black people experiencing varied degrees of harm and disorders, including colonial mentality (Fanon), double-consciousness (Du Bois), inferiority complex (Wa Thiong'o), and epistemic injustice (Ndlovu-Gatsheni). In Ghana, the African Americans I studied enact literate social practices of healing both at a historic site and in their everyday lives to heal from different forms of harm. In this analysis, I categorize these forms of harm into epistemic harm and ontological harm.

Transnational mobility—forced and voluntary—occupies center stage in the denigration and reclamation of Black humanity. From a colonial perspective, the Transatlantic slave trade that forcefully transported enslaved Africans to the now American side of the Atlantic constitutes a damning example of racializing, degrading, and exploiting Black humanity and bodies for the benefit of Western nation-states and corporations. More recently, people of African descent in the diaspora are actively engaging in various practices of healing as decolonial endeavors. Such endeavors have engendered some version of Black/African American transnational mobility to the continent of Africa, especially Ghana. Accordingly, the movement of African Americans from the Global North, the U.S., to the Global South, Ghana, presents a somber epistemic space to account for how individuals in the African American community are constructing radical change by inventing new practices for being and healing transnationally.

Such transnational mobility poses a challenge for decolonial researchers. Methods must attend to how local epistemologies cue literate social practices of transnational subjects returning to their ancestral homeland to experience more just and more dignified versions of being human. In this study I theorize how, in Ghana, African Americans initiate creative literacies shaped by local, Indigenous epistemologies and how our methods can attend to such literacies. These literacies challenge the field's dominant, traditional, and institutional views of literacies. Accordingly, our methods need to account for these unfamiliar, albeit insightful, literacies–situated as they are in spaces embodied by African Americans elsewhere and otherwise. This orientation contributes to several disciplinary conversations.

Literature Review

Rhetorics and Literacies of Healing: Expanding Disciplinary Borders

Research in the discipline has complicated the linear associations of trauma to healing including the fact that joy may be a source of healing. Also, complexities such as the relationship between writer and audience open opportunities for healing. For example, across different disciplines that are concerned with trauma and healing, writing (primarily textual practices of journaling, poetry, and creative nonfiction) has emerged as one of the popular activities that people engage in as an instrument of or on the path to healing (Anderson and MacCaudy; Ryden; Vieira). Over two decades ago, the National Council of Teachers of English published a collection, *Writing and Healing*, edited by Charles Anderson and Marian MacCurdy, that heightened the field's interest in the rhetoric of healing and writing. In her work where she examines the place and dialectic of private and public approaches to healing through writing in the composition classroom, Wendy Ryden suggests that we need to pay "attention to the rhetoric of audience" as "an effective means of showing us the way" in responding to complicated ways through which writing is therapeutic and cathartic. While many studies in the field focus on writing and trauma, Ryden argues that writing to heal should not always emanate from a place of pain; it can also stem from a place of joy or other forms of experiences. Thus, the experiences writers invoke to heal are complicated by the audience, including themselves, with whom they engage in a rhetorical exchange.

The complex somatic dimensions of literacies and healing are conditioned by the way power dynamics override our bodies. At a time when our world continues to experience increasing rates of oppression across many intersectional identities and power imbalances, Kate Vieira in "Writing's Potential to Heal: Women Writing from their Bodies" asserts that we need to further theorize the conditions under which writing as a complex, embodied, and social practice contributes to physical healing (20). In her work with mostly white women seeking physical restoration, Viera theorizes writing as a complex social and bodily practice imbued with the potential to heal people from their physical and emotional traumas. Yet, this access to writing's potential to heal is not available to everyone. That is, it is constrained by people's access to power including ways in which the systems of power that they are exposed to help and privilege their narratives as well as social contexts that afford them the opportunity to use writing to connect their bodies and minds. To account for such unequal access to healing through writing undercut by power and context, as she notes, the discipline needs further qualitative studies that capture the experiences of "diverse groups of writers" (35).

To extend this line of inquiry in the discipline across transnational borders, I contend that we need to theorize other forms of literacies of healing that go beyond writing because writing, itself, is a privileged literacy that may be constrained by power and inaccessible to or uncommon in certain contexts and cultures. Expanding our disciplinary borders to attend to various literacies of healing is critical because there are numerous cultures that use non-alphabetic text and oral practices as methods of healing. In rhetoric and composition scholarship, for example, Iris Ruiz and Sonia C. Arellano theorize medicinal history and quilting as decolonial methods and alternatives of healing from colonial wounds and reclaiming marginalized people's ways of knowing and being in the world.

Ways of Healing in Black Scholarly Writings and Communities

Black scholars across disciplines including literacy studies have theorized various literacy practices and traditions that people of African descent employ towards healing. These scholars demonstrate that healing as a continuing process requires reimagining the traumatic impact of racism on our heads and bodies (Menakem), rethinking what constitutes grief and sorrow within the contexts of systemic oppressions (Wade), and reassessing our thoughts and feelings through embodied mindfulness to increase our emotional resilience (Magee). At its core, knowledge, newly constructed and reclaimed, is the foundation upon which Black people's journey towards healing and reclamation of their humanity rests (Busia). That is, a critical component of such literacy practices and traditions revolves around knowledge-building and learning that center African Indigenous epistemologies, histories, and knowledge of Black people's collective experiences of cultural and epistemic dispossessions (Boutte et al.). Renowned Black literacy scholar Joyce E. King, in what she terms "Diasporan Literacy," argues that one of the ways of healing the souls and minds of Black people is to teach them to appreciate, own, and reclaim their histories and identities as "Africa's children" (321). For King and other scholars, literacy practices including storytelling about the experiences of the African diaspora have the potential to facilitate Black people's capacity to heal by affirming their sense of agency, wisdom, self-recognition, and a repossession of their ancestral/heritage knowledge (King).

Textual practices have afforded African Americans and people of African descent methods of healing. These practices include stories, testimonies, poems, and songs. In many of those practices, the legacy of slavery has been a prominent subject. In the contemporary, Black women writers are exploring "strategies for healing without engaging slavery directly, focusing instead on more contemporary maternal figures…as healers" (Williams 77). For example, this writing documents the healing tradition of laying of hands by the healers who are perceived to possess ancestral spirits similar to priests and priestesses in the African tradition (77). In "Healing Traditions" and *Healing Narratives,* Black scholars Stephanie Y. Evans and Gay Alden Wilentz, respectively, chronicle an array of healing practices such as composing poetry, memoirs, song lyrics, and pursuing cultural reconnection in the writings of Black women writers. Critical in these writings is the function of healing traditions as interventions against mental, emotional, and physical harm perpetrated against members of the Black community.

Further, oral literacies enacted through healing circles constitute a major tradition aimed towards healing in Black communities. Black feminist sociologist Jennifer L. Richardson advances healing circles, in the tradition of African Ring Shouts, as a pedagogical intervention that people of African descent, especially Black women, use to heal. In her research, she theorizes that healing functions as a political and social act of resistance and healing circles allow Black women to create a free space where they can exercise self-care, reflect on their experiences, and build emotional, political, and social bonds to overcome the trauma that media violence has on their humanity (285). Like Richardson, Black psychologist Erlanger A. Turner and others note that emotional emancipation circles are also a type of healing circles with "an African-centered communal cultural orientation" that Black communities use to "target whole communities for healing since racism creates emotional pain and threatens optimal functioning" of Black communities (559). For example, Marc Lamont Hill in his framing of wounded healing suggests that sharing stories of pain and suffering within Black communities and in the classroom creates an opportunity for healing both for the storyteller and the listeners (262). Given that the traumatic experiences emanating from anti-Black racism affect Black communities, these group-oriented healing circles where oral literacies such as storytelling are used emphasize the relevance of community healing as a key component towards the reclamation of Black humanity.

Hybrid Literacies at the Ancestral Slave River Park in Ghana

Given their Western orientation and African heritage, African Americans in Ghana enact hybrid textual and non-textual literate social practices of healing in various local contexts and for various rhetorical purposes. Such practices further complicate both what we constitute as literacies and how we study those practices across diverse communities. As I describe later, a typical example of a context in which African Americans in Ghana exhibit hybrid textual and non-textual rituals of literacies is the Ancestral Slave River Park in the Central Region of Ghana. This is the river site where enslaved Africans captured in the hinterland took their "last bath" before being transported for auctioning. In this context, many African Americans engage in embodied rituals of healing and then later, they write down their names and brief notes on the "Memorial Wall of Return" (Fig. 1).

The Memorial Wall of Return functions as a kind space where African Americans and other Africans in the diaspora symbolically inscribe their names as evidence of their return to their ancestral homeland. This gesture is in defiance of colonial structures that sought to deny them of their right of return home when their ancestors, enslaved Africans, were made to pass through the "gate of no return" before boarding the vessels that took them to the New World. Such complex literate social practices provide insightful cases for us, as scholars, to expand our epistemic borders within community literacy research.

Figure 1: Memorial Wall of Return at the Ancestral Slave River Park in Ghana. Seven concrete slabs stand on an elevated concrete floor surrounded by trees and grass. Beside them is a shorter concrete slab with the inscription "Memorial Wall of Return"

Decolonial Indigenous Methodologies and Methods

Scholars in literacy studies and rhetoric continue to grapple with devising methods that expand and challenge the conventional print and text heavy methods of doing literacy research (Snyder 141-2). Recently, scholars such as Ellen Cushman and Esther Milu, among others have theorized literacy practices from decolonial perspectives that honor various literacies and language practices of Indigenous communities. Such decolonial perspectives challenge us to expand our methods to attend to practices—textual and non-textual—that colonized peoples enact towards decolonizing epistemologies, healing, and other knowledge practices (Browdy and Milu; Mamdani). My methods in this study are informed by Indigenous decolonial approaches (Chilisa; Milu; Smith) for conducting literacy research and community-engaged inquiry among colonized peoples.

The prominent African Indigenous decolonial theorist Bagele Chilisa observes that rediscovery and recovery are critical components of processes of decolonization within Indigenous methodologies because they highlight *how* colonized Others reclaim their histories, cultures, and identities (16). Concerned with how African Americans travel to Ghana to rediscover themselves, reconnect with their ancestral homeland, and recover from the traumas of slavery and anti-Black racism, I employ methods of rediscovery and recovery as they allow me to witness *actual* practices of healing that African Americans enact in their ancestral homeland. Guided by such Indigenous decolonial framework, I go on-the-ground to engage with the local sites in Ghana where African American participants embody and enact varied literacy practices in the service of healing. These methods thus honor African Indigenous methodologies and respond to Browdy and Milu's call for Global Black Rhetoricians to theorize healing in charged sites of trauma such as the Pikworo Slave Camp in Ghana (235) and Mahmoud Mamdani's call for public intellectuals to "be as close to the ground as possible" in doing epistemological decolonial inquiry with local and transnational communities (79).

In our contemporary world where global problems compel peoples to move, travel, and migrate, transnational mobility creates new contexts for writing and demands new literacies (Lorimer Leonard). These realities complicate our methods for doing literacy research. Rhetorician and decolonial methodologies scholar Godwin Agboka has argued that when our participants cross borders into new territories, our methods in decolonial research must adjust to and maneuver around those borders to attend to new questions and account for the practices that our participants engage in within the proper context (319). On the ground, theorizing African Americans' literate social practices in their transnational mobility from the Global North, the U.S., to the Global South, Ghana, presents intricate methodological challenges such as figuring out how to witness firsthand their situated literate social practices at charged cultural sites. As Deborah Brandt and Katie Clinton assert, literacies have the "ability to travel, integrate, and endure" (337) and in the case of African Americans in and visiting Ghana, the creative and situated social literacies that they enact in their travels facilitate their learning, unlearning, and healing.

Methods

Data Collection

I collected data for this study in two ways: first, by observing African American participants at a historic site in Ghana, which included taking photos of literacy artifacts that structured participants' activities at the sites; and, second, by interviewing African Americans about their experiences in Ghana. This two-part approach sought to capture and honor the complex and liberating literate practices of African Americans in Ghana that I became acquainted with as a member of a Facebook group that seeks to provide different resources for African Americans who are visiting or repatriating to Ghana. I learned while participating in this group that in Ghana, African Americans conjure the spiritual and perform varied embodied rituals in real time at charged historic sites and in their daily lives in Ghana. At historic sites such as the Ancestral Slave River Park, I learned that they also infuse these embodied, performative rituals with writing their names and brief notes on site. Based on what I was reading/learning in the Facebook group, I wondered: What is the relationship between these complex and hybrid rituals in relation to African Americans' return to their ancestral homeland? What are these performative rituals and literacies in service of? I was intellectually curious to undertake a study that would systematically theorize the deeper significance of such practices and the methods by which we might study those African-centered practices.

Observing and Engaging Participants at an Historic Site

African Americans regularly visit several historic sites in Ghana. Most of these sites, such as the slave dungeons dotted across the coast of Ghana, Pikworo Slave Camp, and the Ancestral Slave River Park, are connected to slavery while others, such as the Gbewaa Palace and Manhyia Palace, are connected to the richness and dignity of Ghanaian culture. For this study, I traveled to Ghana in the summer of 2022 to observe African Americans' embodied literate social practices at the Ancestral Slave River Park located in the Central Region of Ghana.

On the day I visited the park for my ethnographic observation, I spent about six hours at the site. I first went to the office to introduce myself to the tour guide on duty and explained to him my research objectives for visiting the site, showing him documents such as my student ID and IRB approval from my institution. He gave me consent to participate in and observe activities on site and informed me that he was expecting some visitors on site.

After waiting for some time, I noticed that some minivans carrying visitors had pulled over the parking lot of the site. Most of the visitors were Black. For the entire time, I observed two separate groups of visitors who arrived at separate times. Before the actual "tours" of the site began, the guide on site asked people where they had come from. These organized activities are framed as tours, and I use that language here although it gives me great unease to perceive them as touristic activities. For each of the two groups, many of the people present were from the U.S. and a few were from the Caribbeans, and the U.K. Despite that these other Black diasporans may be returning for similar reasons as African Americans, within the limitations of my study, I focused specifically on African Americans for this research as a case study. I surmise that different Black diasporan communities, given their unique experiences and geographies, may engage in healing practices that account for a particular harm relevant to those unique experiences and we need different studies to theorize similarities and differences in healing practices among Black diasporan communities in and visiting Ghana.

Throughout the tours, I observed certain sequenced activities that cut across many of the African Americans. For example, at the beginning of the trail near what is called the Memorial Wall of Return, as the tour guide told the history of how captured Africans walked barefooted and in chains along the trails to the river for their last bath, I saw several African Americans removing their footwear. Then, they walked barefooted along the trail in moments of silence, being attentive to the history being told. At the river, many of them went down the stairs to the bank of the river that has been designated the "First Bath of Return", stepped into the river, washed their faces and hands from the wrist to the elbow, walked back from the river, walked back still barefooted to the beginning of the trail, and then inscribed their names and brief notes on the Memorial Wall of Return. Among the second group, I observed that a few African Americans shed tears along the way.

During the process, I made notes of these observations in a small notepad and took photos of artifacts without intruding on the personal space of the visitors. At the end, I wanted to hear from participants as they hurried to the tour vans that had brought them to the park. One visitor, Bryt, consented to an interview. She had engaged in all the activities I have described above. She glossed for me the significance of walking to the river and back. In my analysis, I reference her responses regarding the meanings and curative potentials of those literate activities that she performed at the park and her overall travel to Ghana.

For me, these on-the-ground participant observations were significant in three main ways. First, they allowed me to walk alongside African Americans and to bear witness to how their literate social practices embodied their grief and desire for healing in a park memorializing the atrocities and dehumanization that our ancestors were subjected to. Second, this vantage point afforded me opportunities to see the rituals I had read about on Facebook unfolding in time and space in relation to visitors' engagement with and in the park's history. Third, I, too, given my positionalities as Ghanaian and Black, had an embodied experience in solidarity with those with whom I share a common humanity. These experiences informed my coding of the data from the observations and my subsequent interviews with African Americans in Ghana.

Recruiting and Interviewing African American Participants

In addition to Bryt, with whom I had the brief interview at the Ancestral Slave River Park, I recruited the African American participants for this study through Facebook community groups for expatriates in Ghana. I am a member of two closed Facebook groups called "Expat Life Ghana" and "Africans Leaving America." With permission from the administrators, I made a post on the group pages informing members about my study and my search for African American participants. In my post, I invoked our shared history as people of African descent and informed my target audience about how the stories they will share with me will be beneficial to me as an emerging scholar who is dedicating his research to theorizing their insightful practices of healing and decolonial endeavors in Ghana and to the members of the global Black community who have a desire to participate in this communal healing.

After the post, several members indicated their interest in the study and I reached out to them privately. At the time, I was still in the U.S. Given that these were individuals who had agreed to share some of their intimate embodied experiences with me, I wanted to build some relationship and rapport with them over time through regular chat on Facebook. For some, I offered recommendations about strategies for finding accommodation in Ghana, educated them about local fabrics and ethics of dealing with strangers, and suggested other historic places that they may visit to expand their knowledge of cultures in Ghana. When I traveled to Ghana, I met some of the participants including Malik at the W.E.B. Du Bois Memorial Center for Pan African Culture in Accra. My interview with Malik, for example, took place after a month of our in-person meeting. For me, the relationship I built with these participants, some of which moved from the digital space to in-person, increased the level of trust between us and allowed participants to share their deep stories and practices of healing and learning in Ghana with me.

In total, I interviewed 10 participants. While some like Tim and Mia (who has taken an Indigenous name and spells it unconventionally as "Adjua" and not "Adwoa/ Adjoa") have lived in Ghana for a few years, others such as Jeremy and Malik had been in Ghana for less than a month. All the interviews happened over Zoom and, with their permission, I video recorded the interviews in compliance with IRB approval from my university. The interviews lasted between 45 minutes to an hour, and I transcribed the interviews for analysis.

Data Analysis through Grounded Theory and "Sankofa"

I coded the interviews using grounded theory to identify and consolidate themes related to the participants' literate social practices of healing. As a methodology for engaging primary data, grounded theory allowed me to systematically code themes and concepts as they emerged from the data and to render those concepts as analytical narratives to advance the relevant theories I used in this study (Charmaz). Then, I situated those themes that emerged from the data across scholarship on decolonization, epistemic injustice, and ontological denigration of Black being before theorizing the literate social practices of the participants through the lens of Indigenous African concepts and knowledge systems such as Sankofa. Sankofa is an Indigenous Ghanaian philosophical and epistemic concept. Literally, Sankofa is from an Indigenous Akan word that is typically translated as "to return and take it," "to return to your past," or "it is not taboo to go back and retrieve what you have forgotten or lost" (Temple 127). This concept is a practice of intellectual renewal that imbibes in Africans to "learn from or build on the past...in their march forward" (Quarcoo 17). It recognizes the epistemic legitimacy of Indigenous African thought and ways of knowing and advances the need for Africans and people of African descent to repossess all the positive aspects of ancestral and traditional knowledge systems. Christel N. Temple observes that Sankofa, as an African diaspora practice, draws its influences from various perspectives on African consciousness: (a) It is viewed as a heritage of innate cultural behaviors traceable to enslaved Africans and preserved through epic memory by those enslaved Africans who arrived in the Americas; (b) it is considered an act of resistance against Eurocentric knowledge systems and worldviews. Instead, it emphasizes the importance of utilizing African conceptual frameworks to define and characterize contemporary African life; and (c) it also serves as symbolic gestures embraced by Diasporan Africans, signifying a desire for "returning to the source." These gestures represent psychological, epistemic, and ontological steps taken to reconnect with Africanness and embrace their cultural heritage. In my analysis, I show how African Americans in and visiting Ghana embrace this philosophical concept as an intervention towards repossessing their ancestral homeland and heritage knowledge.

Healing from Epistemic Harm: Enacting Travel and Sankofa to Un/Re-learn Black Histories

Sabelo Ndlovu-Gatsheni argues that Western colonial systems and structures constitute a cognitive empire that perpetuates epistemic injustices against Black people through theft and misrepresentation of Black history and epistemological denial of Black civilization and ways of being. In America, such epistemic injustices permeate the educational system, popular culture, and our everyday lives (Maldonado-Torres). In the American educational system, for example, Boutte et al. observe that Black history is taught in ways that misrepresent Black people, beginning their history with slavery and framing continental Africans as savages deserving to be civilized. Such historic and epistemic misrepresentations are not only inaccurate, but they are also unfair in ways that harm the intellectual fortitude and history of Black people within and beyond the American educational system (Boutte et al. 75).

African Americans are actively engaging in healing from these epistemic injustices and harms by exposing themselves to knowledge systems and histories that honor Black humanity and accurately represent the origins of Black histories. In my study, many of my participants decried their experiences of learning about Black histories in school. They noted that the refusal to respect and recognize Black history and ways of knowing contributed to the justification of slavery and significantly perpetuates anti-Black violence and oppression that African Americans continue to experience in the contemporary. Epistemic freedom has thus become a desirable point of healing for African Americans. While all participants had indeed traveled as a source of healing, here I highlight the insights of three participants, Malik, Jeremy, and Bryt, and interpret their insights through the lens of the African concept of Sankofa, "to return and take."

To achieve epistemic freedom and intellectual healing, African Americans embark on traveling to Ghana as a radical literate social act. Given their mistrust of the histories of Black people that they have been exposed to in the American educational system, African Americans travel to Ghana to learn and unlearn the histories of Black people in a socio-historic environment that they regard as credible, experiential, and intellectually empowering. Malik, an African American who has been teaching African American history for over two decades, and whom I met at the W.E.B. Du Bois Memorial Centre for Pan-African Culture, observed that:

> our histories and identities and how we know who we are as Africans, African Americans, or Black people got distorted the very moment our ancestors were captured and forced through the Middle Passage to America. So, for us, it is involuntary travel that resulted in the distortion of our identities and histories. Sometimes, the disease and its cure might come from the same approach, you know. So, I see traveling back to Ghana as a very crucial step towards reclaiming the knowledge about us as people of African descent that has been lost, hidden, or misrepresented...whatever negative word you can use to describe the miseducation about Black history that goes on in America.

Within the context of literacies, travel is a radical literate act in the service of a particular epistemic social action: to un-learn and re-learn Black histories. When Malik conceives "traveling back to Ghana as a very crucial step," I argue that he is framing travel, firstly, as a radical literate act. Secondly, that act is geared towards a goal-oriented social action to reclaim "the knowledge about us as people of African descent that has been lost, hidden, or misrepresented." As a literate act, traveling to Ghana for African Americans becomes a means—a complex literate act that includes all of what is required to undertake a transnational journey—to an end: to reclaim Black histories and humanity. In addition to reading about Ghana, for instance, and writing to set up vaccination appointments and apply for visas to Ghana, etc., African Americans engage with non-textual activities including listening to fellow travelers' recordings on YouTube, Instagram, or Facebook or in conversations when the opportunity arises to hear first-hand about the experiences of other African Americans who have visited Ghana. For example, Jeremy, an African American participant in my study, recounted that listening to his friend Angie tell her story about her "journey through West Africa, Ghana...inspired me to take on a decolonial experience. And I am grateful for that."

From a decolonial perspective, the oral histories and stories told by others such as Angie B. Jones who have visited Ghana constitute literate traditions that create learning moments for people like Jeremy to begin their un-learning and re-learning of Black histories from sources they trust even before they arrive in Ghana. These oral histories and stories are not only consistent with African and African American literate traditions, but they also legitimize the epistemic value of such traditions. In this sense, traveling as a literate act accounts for the complex reading, writing, and exchange of oral histories as, in the words of Malik, a "crucial step" to a broader social action: to un-learn and re-learn Black histories. Thus, for African Americans in Ghana, traveling in all its complexity is a goal-oriented literate act with epistemic potentials in that it sets in motion opportunities to un-learn and re-learn Black histories and by doing so reconciles internal tensions that disturb the mental and intellectual stability of African Americans. At its core, African Americans traveling to Ghana and across Ghana gain experiential knowledge that allows them to not only decolonize epistemologies about themselves but also to challenge biased versions of histories that they have been exposed to and internalized.

When Jeremy visited Ghana, he was struggling with a version of epistemic harm emanating from "the history they told me'" and causing him "anxiety…that hurt" him emotionally and exhausted him physically. He and his wife, who is white, were expecting a baby, and he felt unprepared to teach his daughter the history of their ancestral heritage. He noted that he needed to embark on this journey to "take on a decolonizing experience" and attain "a level of reconciliation and healing" that would prepare him to be a father to a Black girl in America. He made the conscious effort to visit historic cities such as Kumasi, Accra, and Cape Coast in Ghana that are rich in Ghanaian cultures before visiting the slave castles or dungeons. For him, this decolonizing experience allowed him to unlearn the rhetoric that Black history begins with slavery and to re-learn that he shares a "rich rich history" with a "sophistication we were never educated about." Jeremy and others highlight that there is a curative potential in the epistemic-literate work of going on the ground to experience, hear, and recover histories that are told by people who share in and recognize their humanity.

At the Ancestral Slave River Park in Ghana where I met Bryt, she asserted that traveling to Ghana has equipped her with experiential knowledge to challenge widespread claims that Black history started with slavery and also allowed her to reclaim her humanity. Bryt argued that travel is an epistemic-literate social endeavor because:

> knowledge is not only learned in schools or the classroom, you know. You can experience knowledge when you travel. You can see it, feel it. That's what I get from being in Ghana…When I return to America, nobody is going to tell me Black history started with slavery. I have been to Ghana. I have seen the structures of slavery and I have seen the villages and towns, if you like, that existed way before those wicked Europeans reached the shores of Ghana. I have seen the people living in dignity in so many different ways.
>
> You see, I write my name on this wall because I believe my ancestors embodied this space, but they could not leave any traces for us. So, I write my name to remind generations yet unborn that I found my way home on behalf of our ancestors. Today, I have reclaimed their humanity and I hope, in death, they feel at peace.

Across these participants and others, decolonizing the episteme about Black histories is a phenomenological and experiential literate act. It requires traveling and enmeshing oneself into spaces and among people who, as Jeremy puts it, "know their history."

That African Americans enact travel as a path towards healing by reclaiming their histories in their ancestral homeland is consistent with Indigenous Ghanaian concepts of preserving and repossessing knowledge. As African Americans travel to Ghana to reclaim their histories and humanity, they embody and practice the Ghanaian philosophical and epistemic concept of Sankofa.

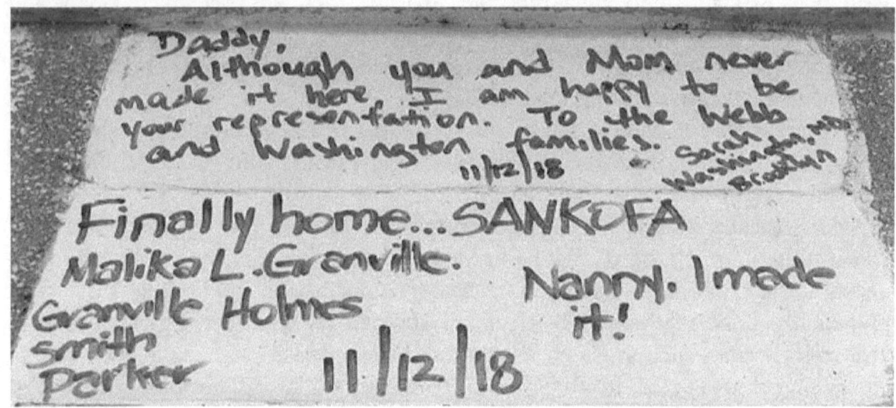

Figure 2: Examples of Inscriptions on the Memorial Wall of Return. Inscriptions such as "finally home," "SANKOFA," and " I made it" are written in black ink with a light orange background on a concrete slab.

As a practice of intellectual renewal, Sankofa as invoked in the artifact above advances an African-inspired philosophical orientation and consciousness that empowers African Americans to return to their ancestral heritage and homelands to reclaim knowledge systems and ways of knowing that reject Eurocentric knowledge systems that denigrate Black histories and humanity. In fact, Black psychologist and scholar Thomas A. Parham observes that Sankofa is applied in Black therapy "to help an individual return intellectually, emotionally, behaviorally, and spiritually to the source of truth, harmony, and spiritual place in their life" (116). Thus, when African Americans reclaim their histories and epistemologies by traveling to their ancestral African roots, the journey has a curative potential of dismantling the cognitive empire that perpetuates anti-Black epistemic harm and injustices that they had been exposed to in the U.S.

Healing from Ontological Harm: Clothing and Naming as Symbolic Literate Acts

On the back of colonialism and on-going coloniality, being Black and human has become an oxymoron. The two cannot or should not co-exist because Western epistemologies equate humanity to whiteness and denigrate Black being. This entrenched epistemic denial of Black humanity and its attendant violent assault on Black lives throughout history and the present is what Calvin Warren terms ontological terror against Black people. Decolonial scholars Walter Mignolo and Catherine Walsh have argued that epistemology frames ontology (106). Thus, Western colonial knowledge and the institutions and structures that sustain such knowledge have framed Black people as non-human or sub-human devoid of a culture and in need of re-humanization through Western civilization. The outcome of such colonial imposition of non-humanness on Black being and the denigration that accompanied it is that Black people suffer from ontological harm.

Ontological harm manifests when people's sense of humanness and being in the world is constantly questioned, denied, and brutalized. Historically, the maltreatment of enslaved Africans through colonialism and the Transatlantic slave trade was a major mechanism through which Black people experienced ontological harm. In the contemporary, widespread racist and anti-Black violence against African Americans in the U.S. are further manifestations of ongoing ontological harm. That is, although there are countless cases of physical violence and painful death that Black people suffer, I contend that such instances of violence are predicated on ontological harm that makes Black lives available for murder and rape in the daily lives of Black people (Maldonado-Torres 255). In fact, Nelson Maldonado-Torres contends that the colonial and racialized invention of blackness in an anti-black world becomes a mechanism through which people of African descent and other colonized subjects consistently experience the denigration of their humanity across different spheres of social, educational, health, and public life.

To heal from ontological harm, African Americans in Ghana are reclaiming their humanity and as Ndlovu-Gatsheni puts it, "forcefully proclaiming… that their lives matter" (896). They are actively enacting various literate social practices aimed at re-humanizing themselves and their families. In essence, they are engaged in an ontological reconstruction and repair to reconcile Blackness and humanness. Such ontological reconstruction is experiential and manifests in intentional everyday literacies of action such as clothing and taking Indigenous names that liberate them from the ontological harm inscribed on their bodies.

Feeling Black and Human in Indigenous African Clothing

Tim, his wife, and son relocated to Ghana in 2019 after witnessing prevalent police brutalities against unarmed Black men and the protests it engendered in the U.S., some of which he participated in. During the interview, Tim told me about how he and his family have embraced wearing Ghanaian made fabrics with African designs as a deliberate practice to value their African heritage and belonging. His rationale for wearing Ghanaian clothing was a direct critique of experiencing the degradation in the U.S. of things African and Black. He said:

> I used to not like wearing them (African designs) as much in the U.S. not to feel real Black…But now, I wear my African print anywhere because now I'm not afraid of standing out. I know there is history; there is a legacy; there

> is richness of culture connected to it. It is a way to bridge the cultural and identity [as Black and human] gap explicitly and externally through clothing.

Clothing becomes a symbolic tool of literacy through which Tim learns to reconstruct and assert his sense of being and feeling Black and human as inseparable. Literacy scholars have theorized that youth from minority populations enact various forms of identities by weaving together literate symbols including clothes "to communicate values, produce meanings, and participate in desired social and cultural communities" (Kirkland and Jackson 279). Indeed, within the African American community and the Black diaspora, "dashiki", an African-inspired clothing, is worn as a cultural symbol of freedom, Pan-Africanism, and global Black solidarity. Given that Tim relocated to Ghana on the back of anti-Black violence against Black people, when he states that he didn't like wearing African clothing in the U.S. in order "not to feel real Black", he is asserting an ontological concern about the possible consequences of feeling real Black in a country that has, as he puts it elsewhere in the interview, "historically oppressed most of the individuals who look like my mother, my father, my uncle, my brother, my cousins."

To highlight the ontological harm of appearing real Black through sartorial representation and the potential anti-Black violence that it may engender, Tim cites recent cases of police brutality against Black people and contrasts that with his experiences in Ghana:

> When you look at stories like George Floyd and so many others, it's hard. But when you come to Ghana, and you know, no matter where you going in the country, generally speaking, unless you open your mouth, no one will know that you are an American. You can go anywhere in the country and no one will call the police because you are a Black man in let's say a fancy neighborhood...In America, to be Black is to be a burden but in Ghana as a Black American, you are the favorite. So, there is a certain level of privilege, so I think you can exist in Ghana without the consciousness that my color is a burden that I have to bear every day. And that in itself is psychologically, emotionally, and spiritually liberating...In Ghana, I don't feel Black. I can simply exist as a human.

The reclamation and proclamation of humanness by Tim are forceful ontological assertions. On the American side of the Atlantic, Black being has been ontologically damaged and brutalized such that it has compelled African Americans to seek to repair and reconstruct their sense of being and humanness on the opposite or African side of the Atlantic. The contrast of being Black on both sides of the Atlantic that Tim expresses accentuates the oxymoronic tension between being Black and human in Western epistemologies and Ghanaian/African epistemologies. For Tim, to be Black in skin color and feel Black through clothing in Ghana is dignifying to his sense of being in the world because it affords him the experience of being treated as a "favorite" and with "privilege", the outcome of which is healing and "liberating."These experiential dynamics of being in Ghana speaks to the healing potential of a mundane act such as clothing when it is intentionally performed as an act of literacy.

Taking Indigenous Names

African Americans in Ghana re-name themselves through adoption of Indigenous Ghanaian names as a literate social practice to re-claim their humanity. Historically, enslaved Africans relied on their literacies of naming practices in Africa to rename themselves in the New World as a form of resisting, "reasserting themselves and reaffirming their humanity in a hostile world" (Mphande 104). Lupenga Mphande further notes that African Americans continue to invoke self-renaming as a social practice to reformulate their identities, reclaim their African heritage, and dismantle "the paradigm that kept them mentally chained for centuries" (104). Several participants noted that they have taken Indigenous Ghanaian names as a form of rebirth and emancipation from the legacies of slavery that desecrated the humanity of their ancestors including changing their names. Adjua was one of such participants.

Adjua, a U.S. military veteran, repatriated temporarily to Ghana in September 2020. Although she travels to the U.S. occasionally, she told me that she has lived much of her life in Ghana since the time she repatriated. A year after repatriating to Ghana, she got "married to a Ghanaian man." Adjua has taken the Indigenous name "Adjua" (common variant spelling include "Adwoa") which is a name given to females born on Monday among the Akan and Fante ethnic groups in Ghana. Adjua asserts that she has taken on this Indigenous name to signal not only her reconstruction of her ontology as a dignified human being of African descent but also to dissociate herself from the legacy of slavery that imposed the names of slave owners on enslaved Africans. She believes that:

> the reason why I want to do that [take an Indigenous name] is because you know, every African American in the States don't have their original last names, okay. We all have slave owners' last name and that's just facts, right? So, when I do this naming ceremony, this is probably the name that I would have been called, maybe if none of that [Transatlantic slavery] had happened. So, it's very important for me to have my own name and not the names that were given to me by a slave master.

Indigenous Ghanaian names perform a spiritual and ontological function in the life of the person so named in the sense that names are believed to influence the person's sense of being in the world. Among the Akans, "Adjua" embodies the Indigenous appellation of "peace" (Agyekum 215). In Ghana, many African Americans take on such Indigenous names during different occasions such as an actual naming ceremony organized by local communities or on Emancipation Day organized by the Ghana Tourism Authority.

In African knowledge systems and worldviews, the essence of a human being is their spirit and names symbolize such spirit (Parham). In *African Names – Reclaim Your Heritage*, Sharon Bernhardt observes that names perform an ontological function in the African worldview because they represent the "person's soul" and not merely "the flesh of the child" (7). Thus, when Adjua renames herself, she is reclaiming her soul, healing from the dehumanizing legacies of slavery, and in essence rehumanizing herself. Although Adjua chose the name "Adjua", she noted that her choice of name was based on "research" on names in Indigenous Ghanaian cultures and the knowledge she has gained from the research has allowed her to enmesh herself into Ghanaian culture given that her husband is Ghanaian. For Adjua and other African Americans in Ghana who have the agency to freely adopt Indigenous names, they heal from the ontological harm that dehumanizes their sense of being in the world through the active literate social practice of Indigenous self-renaming.

Conclusion

For colonized peoples, the place and practices of healing may be conjured in multiple ways including a return to ancestral homelands thousands of miles away and enactment of literate social practices that are in tune with Indigenous epistemologies and local cultures. While undoubtedly scholarship in the discipline has established the curative potential of writing and its limitations within power dynamics, institutional structures, and cultural contexts, African Americans in and visiting Ghana are engaged in literate social practices of healing that challenge us to expand our scholarly borders about literacies and healing as well as to devise emergent methods that honor such practices and the sacredness of the places where such practices are performed.

As African Americans radically pursue healing from the visible and invisible residues of colonialism and ongoing anti-Black violence across transnational borders, they lay bare the complex literacies of healing and the curative potentials of mundane activities such as traveling, wearing clothes, and naming. These literate acts constitute deliberate decolonial endeavors in their performance and effect in that they are geared towards overcoming and liberating African Americans from the epistemic and ontological harms evident in colonial institutions and exploitative anti-Black systems and structures that are manifestly widespread across the U.S.

What is more, African Americans' pursuit of healing in a distant nation-state, Ghana, which has its own capitalist interest in inviting them to return home and invest in its economy, is radical, circumventive, and a refusal to have their pains exploited for economic gains. As evident in my analysis in this study, African Americans in and visiting Ghana rather invest primarily in reclaiming their humanity through healing their bodies, souls, and minds in ways that are experiential and spiritual in performance and epistemically and ontologically liberating in effect. Theorizing such investments in healing foregrounds calls by Black rhetorical scholars for scholars to engage this area of research (Browdy and Milu; hooks). Further, the African-centered and Indigenous practices so enacted by African Americans to heal legitimize the potency of Indigenous decolonial practices of being and knowing (Chilisa; Milu; Smith).

Works Cited

Agboka, Godwin Y. "Decolonial Methodologies: Social Justice Perspectives in Intercultural Technical Communication Research." *Journal of Technical Writing and Communication,* Vol. 44, no. 3, Sept. 2014, pp. 297-327.

Agyekum, Kofi. "The Sociolinguistic of Akan Personal Names." *Nordic Journal of African Studies,* vol. 15, no. 2, 2006, pp. 206-235.

Anderson, Charles M., and Marian M. MacCurdy, editors. *Writing and Healing: Toward an Informed Practice. Refiguring English Studies*. National Council of Teachers of English, 1999.

Attiah, Karen. "Black pain, Ghana's Gain?" *washingtonpost.com*, The Washington Post, 3 Mar. 2023, www.washingtonpost.com/opinions/2023/03/03/tulsa-massacre-survivors-ghana-citizenship/ Accessed 5 May 2023.

Bernhardt, Sharon. *African Names – Reclaim Your Heritage*. Struik Publisher, 2001.

Boutte, Gloria, et al. "Using African Diaspora Literacy to Heal and Restore the Souls of Young Black Children." *International Critical Childhood Policy Studies Journal*, vol.6, no. 1, 2017, pp. 66-79.

Brandt, Deborah, and Katie Clinton. "Limits of the Local: Expanding Perspectives on Literacy as a Social Practice." *Journal of Literacy Research*, vol. 34, no. 3, Sept. 2002, pp. 337-356.

Browdy, Ronisha, and Esther Milu. "Global Black Rhetorics: A New Framework for Engaging African and Afro-Diasporic Rhetorical Traditions." *Rhetoric Society Quarterly*, vol. 52, no. 3, Aug. 2022, pp. 219-241.

Busia, Abena PA. "What Is Your Nation?: Reconnecting Africa and Her Diaspora through Paule Marshall's Praisesong for the Widow." *Changing Our Own Words: Essays on Criticism, Theory, and Writing by Black Women*, edited by Cheryl B. Wall, Rutgers UP, 1989, pp. 196-211.

Charmaz, Kathy. *Constructing Grounded Theory: A Practical Guide through Qualitative Analysis*. Sage, 2006.

Chilisa, Bagele. *Indigenous Research Methodologies*. Sage, 2019.

Clarke, John Henrik. *Christopher Columbus and the Afrikan Holocaust: Slavery and the Rise of European Capitalism*. A & B Books, 1992.

Cushman, Ellen. "Translingual and decolonial approaches to meaning making." *College English*, vol. 78, no. 3, Jan. 2016, pp. 234-242.

Dini-Osman, Ridwan Karim. "'This is where I should be'": 1,500 Black Americans Make Ghana their New Home." *theworld.org*, The World, 7 Sept. 2022, https://theworld.org/stories/2022-09-07/where-i-should-be-1500-black-americans-make-ghana-their-new-home. Accessed 5 May 2023.

Du Bois, W. E. B. *The Souls of Black Folk; Essays and Sketches*. A. G. McClurg, 1903. Johnson Reprint Corp., 1968.

Evans, Stephanie Y. "Healing traditions in Black women's writing: Resources for poetry therapy." *Journal of Poetry Therapy*, vol. 28, no. 3, Jun. 2015, pp. 165-178.

Fanon, Frantz. *The Wretched of the Earth*. Grove P, 1968.

Gaines, Kevin Kelly. *American Africans in Ghana: Black Expatriates and the Civil Rights Era*. UNC Press Books, 2006.

Hill, Marc Lamont. "Wounded healing: Forming a Storytelling Community in Hip-hop Lit." *Teachers College Record*, vol.111, no.1, Jan. 2009, pp. 248-293.

hooks, b. "Representations of Whiteness in the Black Imagination." *Black on White: Black Writers on What it Means to be White*, edited by David R. Roediger, Schocken Books, 2010, pp. 38–53.

Karenga, Maulana. "The Ethics of Reparations: Engaging the Holocaust of Enslavement." *Paper represented at the National Coalition of Blacks for Reparations in America Convention, Baton Rouge, LA*. 2001.

King, Joyce Elaine. "Diaspora Literacy and Consciousness in the Struggle against Miseducation in the Black Community." *The Journal of Negro Education*, vol. 61, no.3, Summer 1992, pp. 317-340.

Kirkland, David E., and Austin Jackson. "'We real cool': Toward a Theory of Black Masculine Literacies." *Reading Research Quarterly,* vol. 44, no. 3, Nov. 2009, pp. 278-297.

Lorimer Leonard, Rebecca. *Writing on the Move: Migrant Women and the Value of Literacy.* University of Pittsburgh Press, 2018.

Maldonado-Torres, Nelson. "On the Coloniality of Being: Contributions to the Development of a Concept." *Cultural Studies,* vol. 21, no. 2-3, Mar./May 2007, pp. 240-270.

Magee, Rhonda V. *The Inner Work of Racial Justice: Healing Ourselves and Transforming Our Communities through Mindfulness*. Penguin, 2021.

Mamdani, Mahmood. "Between the Public Intellectual and the Scholar: Decolonization and Some Post-independence Initiatives in African Higher Education." *Inter-Asia Cultural Studies*, vol. 17, no. 1, Mar. 2016, pp. 68-83.

Menakem, Resmaa. *My Grandmother's Hands: Racialized Trauma and the Pathway to Mending Our Hearts and Bodies*. Penguin, 2021.

Mignolo, Walter D., and Catherine E. Walsh. *On Decoloniality: Concepts, Analytics, Praxis*. Duke UP, 2018.

Milu, Esther. "Hip-Hop and the Decolonial Possibilities of Translingualism." *College Composition & Communication*, vol. 73, no. 3, Feb. 2022, pp. 376-409.

Mphande, Lupenga. "Naming and Linguistic Africanisms in African American Culture." *Selected Proceedings of the 35th Annual Conference on African Linguistics*. Cascadilla Proceedings Project, 2006.

Ndlovu-Gatsheni, Sabelo J. "The Cognitive Empire, Politics of Knowledge and African Intellectual Productions: Reflections on Struggles for Epistemic Freedom and Resurgence of Decolonisation in the Twenty-first Century." *Third World Quarterly*, vol. 42, no. 5, 2021, pp. 882-901.

Parham, Thomas A. *Counseling Persons of African Descent: Raising the Bar of Practitioner Competence*. Sage, 2002.

Quarcoo, Alfred K. *The Language of Adinkra Symbols*. Sebewie Venture, 1972.

Richardson, Jennifer L. "Healing Circles as Black Feminist Pedagogical Interventions." *Black Women's Liberatory Pedagogies: Resistance, Transformation, and Healing within and beyond the Academy*, edited by Olivia N. Perlow et al., Springer, 2018, pp. 281-294.

Ruiz, Iris D., and Sonia C. Arellano. "La Cultura nos Cura: Reclaiming Decolonial Epistemologies through Medicinal History and Quilting as Method." *Rhetorics Elsewhere and Otherwise: Contested Modernities, Decolonial Visions,* edited by Romeo García and Damián Baca, NCTE, 2019, pp. 141-168.

Ryden, Wendy. "From Purgation to Recognition: Catharsis and the Dialectic of Public and Private in Healing Writing." *JAC*, vol. 30, no.1/2, 2010, pp. 239-267.

Smith, Linda Tuhiwai. *Decolonizing Methodologies: Research and Indigenous Peoples.* Bloomsbury Publishing, 2021.

Taylor, Steven JL. *Exiles, Entrepreneurs, and Educators: African Americans in Ghana.* SUNY Press, 2019.

Temple, Christel N. "The Emergence of Sankofa Practice in the United States: A Modern History." *Journal of Black Studies*, vol. 41, no.1, Sept. 2010, pp. 127-150.

Turner, Erlanger A., et al., "Black Love, Activism, and Community (BLAC): The BLAC Model of Healing and Resilience." *Journal of Black Psychology*, vol. 48.no. 3-4, May/Jul. 2022, pp. 547-568.

Vieira, Kate. "Writing's Potential to Heal: Women Writing from Their Bodies." *Community Literacy Journal*, vol.13, no. 2, Spring 2019, pp. 20-47.

Wa Thiong'o, Ngũgĩ. *Decolonising the Mind: The Politics of Language in African Literature.* J. Currey, 1986.

Wade, Breeshia. *Grieving while Black: An Antiracist Take on Oppression and Sorrow.* North Atlantic Books, 2021.

Warren, Calvin L. *Ontological Terror: Blackness, Nihilism, and Emancipation.* Duke UP, 2018.

Wilentz, Gay Alden. *Healing Narratives: Women Writers Curing Cultural Dis-ease.* Rutgers UP, 2000.

Williams, Dana A. "Contemporary African American Women Writers." *The Cambridge Companion to African American Women's Literature,* edited by Angelyn Mitchell and Danille K. Taylor, Cambridge UP, 2009, pp. 71-86.

Author Bio

Mohammed Sakip Iddrisu is a multiple award-winning PhD candidate in the Writng, Rhetorics, and Literacies program at Arizona State University. In his research, he employs Indigenous decolonial methodologies and rhetorical theories to explore rhetorics and literate social practices of resistance, healing, and belonging among minoritized Indigenous, racial, and linguistic populations. To do these, he uses a combination of methods such as qualitative interviews, on-the-ground participant observations, and public discourses across digital spaces to collect and produce data for analysis. His research has been published in *Community Literacy Journal, Teaching/Writing: The Journal of Writing Teacher Education,* and he has a forthcoming co-authored article in *Reflections: A Journal of Community-Engaged Writing and Rhetoric.* He has a chapter in the 2023 edited collection, *A Charge for Change,* published by Parlor Press.

Saliendo del Pueblo: Migration, Literacy, and Non-Literacy Practices in a Mixtec Farmworking Community

Guadalupe Remigio Ortega

Abstract

This article draws from interviews with two Mixtec migrant farmworkers whose life experiences demonstrate how communication, language, and community, across time and borders, impact the ways Indigenousmigrants choose to practice literacy and non-literacy. Using their stories, I disrupt and decenter the Western definition of literacy and instead present it as a tool for discrimination that erases the Latinx Indigenousvoices, knowledge, and ways of being by replacing it with reading and writing. Instead, I introduce non-literacy as a representation of positive and proud oral traditions that counter the many effects of discrimination. Moreover, non-literacy helps us understand how oral Indigenousmigrant communities make the choice to prioritize the orality of their culture even when surrounded by reading and writing. This approach offers a more appropriate and respectful way to understand how oral Indigenouscommunities choose to live and make sense of the world around them.

Keywords: communication, community, literacy, non-literacy, illiteracy, language, migration

Introduction

In this article, I write the story of my mother and father and the ways in which they have practiced communication, language, and community over time and across borders. Their stories and life experiences demonstrate resistance, renewal, and Indigenouspride (Jackson and DeLaune 46; Lyons 449; Powell 400) and help us reimagine community literacy as a conscious and collective practice where individuals and groups make specific choices as far as how, when, and why they want to use literacy and non-literacy. As a Mixtec scholar, I frame and discuss literacy based on my experience growing up in a primarily oral community where I have seen, through my parents' examples, the intentional choice to practice non-literacy rather than literacy. This choice is seen in that my parents continue to prioritize non-literacy even after 50 years of being part of literate communities that practice reading and writing.

As I started thinking about the definition and value of literacy in my own community, I attempted to fit our cultural and linguistic practices into the ever-expanding definition of literacy (Street 47) but eventually realized that this was not necessary. Instead, I am choosing to define literacy as the act of using reading and writing to communicate with others to make sense of our surroundings. Equally important to my framing of literacy is my definition of non-literacy or, "the intentional, conscious, and continuous decision to not use literacy, but rather prioritize orality, human connection, stories, spirituality, and connection to land to communicate with others and make sense of our surroundings." Non-literacy reflects the *choice* to not use or value literacy as we see it in the Western (American) tradition; the prefix *non* implies the choice and the distinction our community is making between the literacy practices of the US and the practices we use as a community. In considering these definitions, it is just as important to understand that while complex cultural, legal, economic, and technological forces greatly influence who can choose literacy or non-literacy in any given context, studying the tensions migrants experience between these two poles helps us understand how such forces can arise from the effects of colonialism and discrimination, as has been the case in my community. When listening to my parents' stories, it is clear that cultural and economic forces, often put in place by the effects of colonialism, such as poverty and the need to salir del pueblo, influenced the choices they and our community made. Ultimately, the culmination of these effects and choices resulted in the forced migration that eventually brought them to the US. While they were sometimes forced to make decisions regarding literacy and non-literacy practices, they always did so with an understanding of the consequences of doing so. My parents and El Pueblo de San Miguel Cuevas, my parents' village in Santiago Juxtlahuaca, Oaxaca, have actively made the conscious decision to use both literacy and non-literacy even while navigating and being part of literate spaces since their migration out of San Miguel Cuevas. In most instances, they have chosen to prioritize non-literacy using the oral and spiritual practices of our ancestors, land, and Mixtec knowledge. In an act of radical imagination, I am disrupting and decentering the Western definition of literacy; instead I view the Western notion of literacy as a tool for discrimination that erases the Latinx Indigenousvoices, knowledge, and ways of being by replacing it with reading and writing. For this reason, I am reclaiming non-literacy to represent positive and proud oral traditions that counter the many effects of discrimination. This transforms non-literacy into a positive, intentional, and proud choice, an act of self-preservation and resistance. Through observing my community, I have come to see how, by Mixtec standards, literacy's history as a tool of discrimination is unnecessary and not needed to communicate, thrive, and be in the world. Even after obtaining the skills to read and write in Spanish or English, El Pueblo has repeatedly chosen not to use those skills but rather, has often chosen non-literacy to navigate this world.

In my research, I make the distinction between literacy and non-literacy because of the historical oppression and discrimination associated with the former as seen in colonialism and current issues surrounding migration. Current scholarship in literacy studies defines literacy opportunity as "people's relationships to social and economic structures that condition chances for learning and development" (Brandt 7). Using this, I draw upon Brandt's concepts of literacy opportunity and sponsors to explain how literacy in migrant farmworking communities is primarily used by non-migrants to exploit migrant farmworkers. Additionally, scholarship in literacy studies, anthropology, and migration studies including De Genova's use of "capital" and "workplace literacies" (423), Stephen's "cultural citizenship" (231), and Horton's "identity loan" (13) helps us understand how in the present-day literacy continues to be used as an Eurocentric tool of oppression and discrimination. Literacy is seen as a reward and privilege demonstrating the coercion of literacy and the power relations it brings to light for migrant farmworkers (De Genova 423). Similarly, literacy is exploitation through employer surveillance and farmworkers' vulnerability (Horton 15). Other scholarship sees literacy as access, citizenship, and membership which leaves migrant farmworkers struggling to demonstrate their own part as members of society even after being in the US for decades (Ribero 31; Stephen 231; Varsanyi 299; Vieira 1; Wan 38). In this way, seeing literacy as a positive, sometimes defined as "empowerment" begs the question—who is empowered and who is disempowered by this? Throughout history, "literacy as empowerment" has only hurt Indigenouscommunities by forcing them to acquiesce to the dominant group and in doing so has contributed to the erasure of Indigenousidentity and knowledge (Rios 60). Scholars on Indigenous-Studies have focused on survivance, survival, and sovereignty as a way to highlight resistance and pride (Gilmore and Wyman 121; Lyons 499; Powell 400) giving us an alternative to literacy. In our efforts to reclaim our Mixtec identity and deconstruct European notions of Indigeneity, we choose non-literacy and bring to the front our Indigenousvalues and knowledge.

The literacy and non-literacy practices of my parents serve as an example and catalyst for reimagining community literacy by observing and learning from Indigenousmigrant communities such as El Pueblo. When I write "El Pueblo," I am referring to both the physical land of San Miguel Cuevas (in the context of Mexico) as well as the group of people that make up this community (in the context of being in the US). In this article, I take a closer look at what literacy means in the context of modern conversations in literacy studies, contemporary Mixtec culture, and the intersectionality of those concepts. My research questions include:

1. How are transnational Mixtec literacy and non-literacy practices shaped through journeys of migration?
2. How does understanding non-literacy help us understand how oral communities such as El Pueblo choose to use reading and writing as a tool throughout their migrant journey?

Understanding El Pueblo and Acknowledging My Positionality

The Mixtec are the third largest Indigenousgroup in Mexico coming from the region of La Mixteca which crosses the southern states of Oaxaca, Guerrero, and Puebla. The Mixtec speak Mixteco, a language composed of a range of 30-50 dialects, some very distinct, which means it's possible for two neighboring pueblos to not be able to understand one another. Mixteco is to this day mostly and primarily an oral language.

Although there have been efforts to write the language, this has been extremely challenging due to the many dialects that make up the language. The Mixtec of San Miguel Cuevas identify as Catholic, resulting from the forced conversion to Christianity with the arrival of the Spaniards. However, despite this forced conversion,the Mixtec have been able to hold on to their spiritual practices comprised of a mix of Catholicism—we baptize infants, we celebrate first communions, and celebrate El Día de la Virgen de Guadalupe—while continuing our practices of animism including relying on curanderos and limpias, honoring our dead, and caring for our land.

Although El Pueblo has been in the US for over 60 years, we have struggled to build a positive relationship with Western literacy practices. This is the result of ideologies and movements which place a higher value on literacy while pushing aside and demeaning oral practices as illiterate (Garcia Cifuentes 5; Goody and Watt 307; King 2). We should also note that Indigenousknowledge and Mixtec spirituality cannot be replaced with, nor do they neatly fit in with Western definitions of literacy. For example, even after centuries of having been colonized by the Spaniards, El Pueblo continues to practice a form of syncretism—a small Catholic church is located in the center of San Miguel Cuevas while simultaneously Mixtec curanderos continue to do limpias and ofrendas in el monte praying for the land and rain to bless us. Literacy and non-literacy practices in El Pueblo have changed over time and across borders as demonstrated by my parents and their community of San Miguel Cuevas through their ability to employ and utilize reading and writing to their advantage. When migrating to the US their non-literacy is complicated when they begin to use more traditional forms of literacy (Purcell-Gates 68; Stephen 235). For example, although non-literacy continues to be their primary practice of communication, the community comes to see the need and benefit of using reading, writing, and speaking Spanish (or English). Doing so makes it easier to access housing, enroll their children in public schools, head start, and find employment in migrant work camps. There are, of course, ways around this. For example, we continue to see migrants helping each other out by reading, writing, and speaking on behalf of those who are less literate in Spanish and/or English.

Now that I've shared a brief description of who the Mixtec are, I would like to acknowledge my positionality as a college-educated, English and Spanish speaking member of the Mixtec community. My Abuelita spoke only Mixtec her entire life, never learned to read or write, and never left her small home in El Pueblo. She passed away in 2015 and was buried in San Miguel alongside my Abuelito. My father did not have formal schooling and my mother has a 3rd grade education. This is the reality for most members of El Pueblo. My parents' generation have on average a 3rd grade education, but most in my generation born or brought to the US as children have attained a high school diploma. Although my upbringing and exposure to literacy differs greatly from that of my parents and grandparents, I acknowledge that the voices and stories of El Pueblo have a lot to offer us today as we reconsider what literacy means and why it's valued. As a member of El Pueblo, but also as someone raised in the US, there are things that I hear and learn from these stories that I can pass onto readers outside our community while still acknowledging the difficulties of comprehending these practices. My own experience as someone who is literate and educated have prompted and guided me through this research—awareness of what literacy is has provided me with the capability to write this article, while the limits of literacy have moved me to acknowledge my parents' ways of communication, language, and community as Indigenousknowledge unattainable through Western literacy practices.

Methodology

In May 2022, I traveled to Fresno, California, to visit family and to carry out in-person interviews for my dissertation. I decided it was important to spend a couple of weeks casually conversing with my parents about my project—what I was doing, why I was doing it, what it would look like, and how it was part of my PhD studies. For the first time in the past 12 years of my college and graduate schooling, they were beginning to understand my work and research. I began the interviews by going over the IRB consent forms in Spanish, explaining to them what these were and what they meant and sharing with them how the interview would be carried out. I emphasized they should view this as a conversation rather than an interview and informed them I would be audio recording our conversations for the purpose of being able to come back to them, listen, take notes, and write about what they were sharing with me.

My mother was nervous from the start. She said, "Tu nos dices que vamos a decir." For many years my parents have relied on my siblings and me to speak for them—most of the time we've translated their words and the words of others for them. We've done this in public places such as hospitals and schools as well as over the phone, for example when setting up a doctor's appointment. We've also translated correspondences, such as letters in the mail that they didn't understand. We've also spoken Spanish on their behalf in settings where they were not able to understand more formal Spanish words or technical jargon. For a large part of my life, they have looked to me to help them say what they need to say when speaking with those who are not part of our community. This interview was the first time they've been asked to share their stories, in their own words and in a more casual setting. My mom's nervous response is an example of how many Indigenouscommunities in the US perceive themselves to this day. Colonialism, social prejudice, and discrimination, both in Mexico and the US, labels them as inferior and/or illiterate, which makes them afraid to speak, especially in their home language (King 10; Stephen 300). The demanding and withholding of literacy experienced by Indigenouscommunities with the arrival of the Spaniards has contributed to this feeling of fear and inferiority, and I can see how it continues to impact Mixtec migrants such as my mother.

I decided to use my parents' stories in this article as a way to honor and respect them—my parents are elders of the community; their knowledge and stories are tenets of the foundations of El Pueblo. Although in the US our parents and grandparents come to us for help translating English, we know their place in society is above ours given their age, wisdom, and experiences. I begin with my father's first journey saliendo del Pueblo in 1967 to find work in the state of Morelos where he is exposed to Spanish for the first time and learns how to speak, read, and write it. Before this, non-literacy was his only way of life, as is the case for most Mexican Indigenous-communities in southern Mexico. In fact, at this time there are few individuals in El Pueblo who speak, read, and write Spanish; this is a new practice and is mostly used to communicate with city officials in Juxtlahuaca for the purpose of birth and death records and the little government (financial) assistance provided to Indigenouscommunities. Outside of that, El Pueblo continues to operate and thrive through their oral language and spiritual practices much like they did pre colonialism, once again demonstrating resistance and Indigenouspride. Following my father's story, I offer a shorter section on my mother's journey saliendo del Pueblo, which begins before she is even born when my Nana and Tata (maternal grandparents) migrate to La Junta, Oaxaca, in 1962.

In my parents' experience, and as seen across El Pueblo, literacy is at times defined as the ability to read, write, and speak in Spanish and after migration to the US, doing so in English. Other times, literacy is defined as the ability to speak Spanish, and with migration to the US, in English. There are certain values placed on one's ability to speak Mixteco versus Spanish and English. The expectations to speak, read, and write Spanish are barriers my parents have faced since they set foot outside El Pueblo and began to encounter non-Indigenouscommunities first in Mexico and eventually in the US.

Saliendo Del Pueblo

My father has always been a storyteller. He can recall every significant moment of his life with dates, locations, and vivid details. His story begins in 1958 when he is 5, and my Abuelita takes him to the local schoolhouse to enroll him in kindergarten. The teacher, however, says my father cannot stay since only children 6 years old and older are able to enroll in school. He returns home in tears knowing he has to wait a whole year before he can attend school. The following year my Abuelito passes away unexpectedly, and unfortunately, my Abuelita can no longer take my father to the schoolhouse. Instead, she finds work in el monte (the countryside) and takes my father with her. For many years, work has been limited in El Pueblo—you either become a farmer and sell your produce and meat in La Plaza (farmer's market) in Juxtlahuaca, you set up a small store in the village, or you leave El Pueblo to find work elsewhere. The work my Abuelita and father find is always manual field work usually cutting up sugar cane or harvesting fruits or vegetables. It is not a stable, consistent work. Instead, they work for a couple of days and then wait several more days before they can get someone else to pay them to work again.

For many years, as far back as I can remember, my father has always told us the story about getting sent home by the schoolteacher and how he is never able to return. It's not until now however, that I begin to question why this is such a memorable moment for my father. Out of all his childhood experiences, this is the one he remembers and chooses to share most often. This could be because of its close timing to my Abuelito's passing or it can also be because he has come to wonder how his life might have been different had he been able to go to school. He acknowledges the benefits of formal schooling. Perhaps because he has seen how it has benefited his children. Or perhaps because he himself has used reading and writing to his advantage. Yet, as a result of having no formal schooling, his non-literacy has become stronger, and he continues to be a community leader and storyteller in his native Mixtec. Growing up in El Pueblo, my father knew the one-room schoolhouse was a place where you went to learn, but he also came to realize that he was able to do well in his community without this formal education, at least in the land of San Miguel. It seems literacy, defined as reading and writing, was not the focus of his community, but rather formal education and literacy were equated to work, and if one could work and live well without reading and writing, then that was just fine. Today, many parents in my community tell their children, "You either do well in school or you go to work with me." It seems both work and school have equal value for many of us.

My father 's first language is Mixteco Bajo. Most of the small villages in La Mixteca speak an Indigenous language—Mixtec, Zapotec, and Triqui being the most well-known and documented. In 1968, at the age of 14, my father left El Pueblo on his own and traveled to Morelos, Mexico, to work. In Morelos, he heard Spanish for the first time. He finds work in the fields earning 10 pesos al día. On the first day of work, the mayordomo explains to him what he has to do and how to do it. Unable to understand the instructions given to him in Spanish, my father stands there motionless; the mayordomo then returns when he realizes my father does not understand the language:

> Que se viene el señor pa' donde estoy. Llegó donde estoy y—es buena gente, no me regañó, no nada. Ya sabía que no—se dio cuenta que no hablaba yo español. Él lo que hizo agarró una planta y empezó a mocharle las hojas. Nomás dejaba dos ramitas, lo más tiernito la punta. Me dijo el señor que así lo quería. Entonces ya empecé, con las señas nomás, empecé a trabajar. (Remigio Luna)

Through signs and hand gestures, my father is eventually able to understand what he is supposed to do and little by little he begins to pick up Spanish words. The more he hears the language and the more he interacts with the other farmworkers, he begins to make sense of the words and phrases: "This is what you say in order to get this. If you have a question about an assignment, you say this____. When greeting someone, you say this _____." Spanish becomes a requirement and a tool for survival since he has to speak it to be able to work and move around in this part of Mexico where most people do not identify as solely Indigenousnor speak an Indigenouslanguage, much less speak the Mixtec dialect of his hometown.

Finding Work (and Literacy) Away from Home

Before my mother was born, my Nana and Tata migrated to La Junta, Oaxaca (about 12 hours away from El Pueblo). As she recalls her childhood, my mother shares: "Mis papas iban y venían. Yo, lo que me recuerdo más es cuando ya tenía seis años, me metieron a una escuela, primer grado. Duré en ese lugar donde vivimos, creo que duramos como yo en la escuela unos cinco, seis meses en primer año." Similar to my father's family, my mother and her family were forced to leave El Pueblo because there was no work there. By now many have come to realize that in order to survive with a family, you have to leave El Pueblo and travel to the surrounding cities and states to find work and sustenance. This movement started out slowly many decades ago and explains the migrant lifestyle my mother's family lived.

During my mother's early years, my Nana began to work lavando ajeno. She is able to find this type of work due to her ability to speak and communicate well in Spanish. She realizes her Spanish literacy is a skill and tool that can provide work opportunities outside the fields, so when my mother is 12, my Nana finds her work as a maid. Similar to my father, my mother's continuous exposure to literacy occurs in the workplace, away from her hometown. Here she starts to learn about household appliances she didn't know existed. She is used to washing her clothes and that of her siblings in the canal. Here she learns how to wash the family's clothes in their wringer washing machine. She learns to read more Spanish since she has to read instructions for the different tasks she has to do during the day. She finds herself speaking Spanish more often. Also, her Spanish needs to be more formal and her vocabulary more advanced. As with any other language, vocabulary, tone, and formality change depending on the setting and environment. Living with a non-Indigenous and more well-to-do family, my mother's literacy practices manifest differently than when she is at home with her parents and siblings, where she rarely uses reading and writing and instead communicates primarily in spoken Mixtec and at times in Spanish. This literacy begins to influence her behavior and her understanding of the world (Brandt 567), especially as they apply to social classes and hierarchies. This is the beginning of my mother's perception of what it means to be poor versus rich, and she begins to form a mentality that language, ethnic background, skin color, and class make one person superior to another. I still see a lot of this manifested in the way she speaks and presents herself today. For example, as previously mentioned, when we started this interview, she seemed nervous and hesitant and indicated that I should tell her and my father what to say. She sees herself as different and less intelligent than the gente fina she is working for. The appliances they use and their lifestyles are foreign to her, in this case due to a lack of income. The way she comes to understand it, a person with money and education, una persona de letra, is perceived as being better than a persona del campo, although in this comparison, the imbalance is in financial possessions rather than in literacy. Ultimately, what she is exposed to and what she comes to see as the norm is that being a persona de letra entails having education, wealth, and literacy (all collapsed into one another), a direct opposition to a persona del campo.

As has been demonstrated, my parents' childhood and upbringing determined the ways they were exposed to literacy and how they used this as a tool to their advantage. What I mean here is that while they both continued to practice and prioritize non-literacy, they were also attentive to what they needed to do to navigate the literate workplaces they became a part of. One could argue my mother had it better: she didn't have to work in hot weather, exposed to the elements like farmworkers. She had consistent pay and a somewhat secure job; yet her choice to leave this in order to be with her family even if it meant working in the fields and earning less demonstrates how literacy is not always a path to upward socioeconomic mobility. Literacy does not always benefit everyone equally, and in fact for some, including Indigenous communities, the harm is much worse than any temporary benefits. This is demonstrated when we compare my father's family (all native Mixtec speakers) and my mother's family (fluent Mixtec and Spanish speakers). Whereas my father moved out of El Pueblo and started to learn Spanish at 14, my mother grew up with both Spanish and Mixteco. Both of her parents spoke both languages and she mostly used Spanish in the various households she worked in. However, she too did not find reading and writing a necessity, at least not beyond the ability to be able to read instructions in the homes where she worked and signs in the city where she lived. Through all this, her family continued to face discrimination and prejudice because they were indigenous, and eventually, they made the decision to only speak Spanish, and not Mixteco, as a way to better fit in and be treated more fairly. As her story demonstrates, with literacy being a tool for discrimination, it didn't matter much that my mother and her family spoke Spanish; it was very clear to non-Indigenous groups that they were Indigenous due to their distinct features and Mixtec-speaking practices. Although being literate in Spanish had helped their financial situation somewhat, there is a lot literacy wasn't able to and couldn't do for them.

Both my mother's and father's stories and experiences with Spanish literacy demonstrate the need to complicate how we understand and value literacy alongside non-literacy in Indigenous communities such as the Mixtec. Through their experiences and reflections, my parents' stories make important contributions to literacy studies and transnational migration studies because their experiences show how we need to reimagine new ways of understanding community literacy and non-literacy alike. Their ability and choice to move back and forth between literacy and non-literacy demonstrates their conscious decision to use literacy as a tool while maintaining a strong identity and place in their Mixtec community.

Literacy and Non-Literacy in Transnational Migration

After listening to and reflecting on my parents' stories growing up and leaving El Pueblo, I found it necessary to go back and discuss with them their thoughts and experiences with literacy and non-literacy, more specifically, as well as how that compares to the ways they make sense of the world in the context of migration. I asked them a variation of the following questions:

1. ¿Qué idiomas habla? ¿Qué idiomas lee o escribe? ¿Con qué idiomas se siente más cómodo en casa, en el lugar de trabajo, en la tienda u otros lugares públicos, etc.?
2. ¿Puede contarme cómo usted se comunica con otros y cómo entiende sus alrededores (físico, espiritual, y trascendente)?
3. ¿Cuáles son algunas prácticas espirituales relacionadas a su identidad y experiencia Mixteca en El Pueblo ? ¿En los Estados Unidos?

4. ¿Cómo ha utilizado, o como le ha ayudado usar, la alfabetización tradicional (lectura (leer) y escritura (escribir)) como trabajador agrícola migrante?

With these questions, my focus was to further understand their linguistic practices and how their use of Spanish and Mixtec has changed over the years from when they first left El Pueblo to their time migrating to the US and being unable to return to El Pueblo. As a primarily oral community, I wanted to learn how they use language and community to understand their surroundings.

Learning to Write in the Fields

n 1969, my father makes his first trip to Sinaloa. At this time, he speaks Spanish, not fluently, but he is able to carry a conversation, at least in the workplace—how do I get work? Who is hiring? What do I need to do to get the job? What does the job consist of? He shares that even today he doesn't speak Spanish "muy bien, pero como quiera lo entiendo y lo que hablo la gente me entiende." My father and I have spoken Spanish with each other my whole life; I am currently 32 years old. There's only 1 word that I've heard him mispronounce. When he wants to say "diferencia" (difference), he says "referencia" (reference). Other than a couple slight accent changes, I would say my father is a fluent Spanish-speaker even though he would say otherwise. Many struggle to learn a second language, but he has been able to learn Spanish despite its vast difference to Mixteco. He was however forced to learn this new language and through time he's been made to believe the Spanish language is superior to his native tongue. I continue by asking him how he learned to read and write in Spanish:

> Allá en Sinaloa, en—No me acuerdo, alguien puso así, escribió mi nombre. Y nomas lo grabé en cómo está la letra, ¿no? Pero no lo pude grabar qué letra es. Nomás de seña, cómo está y así hacia yo en el—Después hasta el 77, cuando yo estaba aquí en Estados Unidos, entonces, ahí unos los compañeros me enseñaron cómo voy a hacer mi nombre y cada letra cómo se llama. Ahí empecé poco poquito a grabar las letras de mi nombre y de mi apellido. Empecé a hacer un poquito—Hasta ahí, pero hasta el 77. Ya tenía como 24 años. (Remigio Luna)

At 24 years old, he learns the alphabet and notices the usefulness of knowing and understanding each letter. I would like to point out that at 24, my father had been speaking Spanish for 10 years; and yet, he continued to make the conscious decision to only use it in the workplace and only when absolutely necessary.

Before this he knew how to write his name only through memorization but couldn't say which letter was which or what sound each one made. With this new knowledge, he is now able to form words and write things beyond his first and last name. As he continues to practice his spelling and letter-writing, he begins to write personal letters (in Spanish) to send to my Abuelita in El Pueblo. During this time there are no personal phones, so letter writing becomes a more accessible form of communication although not always the primary way. My father continues going to the caseta once every couple of weeks to make phone calls, but letter writing provides a more affordable way to communicate. The purpose of these letters is mostly to say hello, see how she is doing, and update her on his well-being. He describes his writing process as follows: "A veces sobraba letra, a veces hacía falta. Batallé mucho y luego pues ya no le eché más ganas, hasta ahí nomás." He writes and sends letters to my Abuelita who then finds someone in the village who is literate in Spanish. They read or sometimes simply summarize the letter to her. Then, she asks them to help her write a letter to return to my father. During this time, this is how they practice literacy to communicate with one another while my father is in the US.

Today, my father describes his reading and writing abilities as "muy despacio," too slow. He struggles with sounding out the letters especially when encountering new words or words that are not part of his daily vocabulary. Yet, what some would consider to be a disadvantage, my father sees as simply a *choice*—as a migrant farmworker, he *chose* to prioritize his Mixtec orality and work to support his family. He *chose* not to continue to practice his reading and writing mostly because he did not deem this as necessary. As far as his writing: "Escribo pero no escribo bien, bien. A veces no pongo la letra, lo que se necesita, pongo otras. Es lo que sé, pues gracias a Dios de que aprendí algo, porque como le digo, no fui a la escuela" (Remigio Luna). He recognizes he knows the basics and is grateful for that since he didn't go to school. But he also mentions that he doesn't always write the right letters or sometimes he doesn't write them correctly, but his reading and writing have definitely grown with his time in the church. Before joining the protestant church, he read very little. However, once he became a member of the church, he is required to read 3-4 times during the week at church. Reading at home is greatly encouraged, and oftentimes they have monthly gatherings where the Bible is read. My father's need to read and write in Spanish increases immensely. This is just one example of how the value of formal schooling has changed in my community over time. With migration to the US and more of us graduating high school and going to college, we've adapted to different lifestyles and jobs. For my Abuelita, and her generation, who lived in El Pueblo most of her life, formal schooling was a luxury rather than a need. For my father's generation, being in the US and becoming part of other communities has pushed them to read and write more, allowing them to see and experience some of the benefits of literacy (Kalmar 5), all while continuing to prioritize their Mixtec identity by choosing non-literacy.

I ask my father if prior to learning to write his name, was it necessary or required for him to sign his name at work. He shares:

> En el 72 estuve trabajando un tiempo en Hermosillo, no mucho tiempo. Ahí sí ocupaba firma para que nos pague. Cada persona que va saliendo su nombre, tiene que firmar y ya le dan su dinero. Salió mi nombre y le dije, "No sé firmar."
>
> Entonces el pagador me dijo, "Espérate hasta el último." Me hice a un lado, llamaron a otro, firmó y ya le pagaron. Llamaron a otro de allá de San Miguel. También igual que yo, no sabía hacer su nombre. También lo hicieron para atrás. Pagaron toda la gente ya el último, entonces nos pagaron a nosotros, yo y a aquel otro hombre. Lo que hicieron, con lapicero estuvieron

> raspando aquí en el fondo de mi dedo, el dedo grande. Ya le mancharon todo aquí. Después dijeron que ponía huellas y medio quedó ahí no era pues tinta. Entonces me pagaron. Entonces sí, es muy importante aunque no sabe mucho, pero con el que sepa hacer el nombre, sí es de bastante ayuda.

In this example, my father becomes more aware of the importance of literacy in the workplace. He needed to at least be able to sign his full name, something he wasn't able to do prior to 1977. He is able to get employment and even get paid, but it is an inconvenience and one that is not as easily accommodated. Being able to write your full name was the most basic and important thing you needed to be able to do to get around. Even my Abuelita who never learned to read or write said this (in Mixteco): "Con que sepa uno escribir su nombre, con eso está bien." My father shares how for several years, writing was not necessary to be able to work. On multiple occasions when he did not know how to write or sign his own name, the mayordomo had my father use his fingerprint in order to "sign" that he had received his paycheck. Only after doing this, would he get paid. After it became too difficult with not knowing to write his own name, he sought out someone to help him learn. For my father, learning to write his name was not only the first step, but also the only thing he needed at the moment. It takes my father 10 years of knowing Spanish and working in a non-Mixtec environment before there is a need for him to learn to write. Writing began with memorization and copying letters. At the time he didn't know that the letter P was called P or that it made a specific sound. The only thing he needed to know was that that was the first letter of his first name and that it was shaped like this: "P." For him, writing (literacy) is important, but not always necessary. We see this when he describes his literacy skills: "Batallé mucho y luego pues ya no le eché más ganas, hasta ahí nomás." Here my father is emphasizing the choice he made to not continue using literacy but instead make non-literacy a priority in his life. He acknowledges his struggle in learning to write while pointing out it was his choice to stop and not continue the practice.

Literacy as a Tool

By 1977, my father had known Spanish for 10 years. He now spoke the language pretty well but only when needed at work. Given that many of his co-workers were also from San Miguel, he only needed to speak Spanish with his superiors—mayordomos and patrones. Mixteco continues to be his preferred language of communication and given that this is solely an oral language, my father, and the entire people of San Miguel, do not see the need to read or write unless of course it is needed to communicate with non-Mixtec peoples (Hernandez-Zamora 7). Instead, culture, law, and wisdom are all passed down orally and spiritually. My father's knowledge and the way he understands the world around him is a result of what he has learned from his parents and elders in his community. Generations before him are able to survive and thrive without the need to read or write (Goody and Watt 310). In fact, all of his experiences with speaking Spanish, as well as reading and writing, occur outside San Miguel. My father describes his current reading level as "muy despacio," too slow due to his struggle with putting letters together. He describes his writing as "no muy bien." Sometimes he misses letters, sometimes he puts the wrong letters, yet he expresses gratitude to God given that although he didn't go to school, he was able to learn to read and write (Garcia Canclini 20). A "skill" and tool which was never a concern to his parents or grandparents has become something he is grateful for (Kalmar 10), yet this only becomes obvious to him once he leaves San Miguel and encounters how non-Mixtec communities enact literacy, what they value, and why it's viewed as a necessary skill. Although El Pueblo has done well historically, not becoming fluent in speaking, reading or writing Spanish or English, as is the case for many Mixtecs now in the US, is seen as a negative trait and continues to bring about discrimination and oppression. This is why we need to understand non-literacy as the intentional choice to reclaim and demonstrate our orality and Indigenousknowledge rather than always placing literacy on a pedestal.

Reading, Writing, and Spoken Language

On the other hand, my mother doesn't remember which language she learned to speak first, but she does know she was speaking both Mixteco and Spanish by the time she was 6 years old. Both her parents were bilingual. My Nana's father, Luis Galindo, was bilingual as well, so unlike my father, my mother's side of the family consists of several generations of Spanish speakers. My mother can read and write in Spanish which she learned when she started school as a child. She considers herself to be a better reader than writer saying she doesn't write "correctly" in reference to sentence structure and grammar. She knows all the letters of the alphabet but struggles with writing them correctly or spelling words right. She started school at 6 years old, first grade, but as her family moved homes, her schooling was severely interrupted. She remembers not finishing first grade by the time she started second grade and similarly before starting third grade. By the time she started third grade, the school year was almost over. After third grade, she was not able to continue since the schoolhouse was only up to that grade. If she wanted to continue, she had to attend the schoolhouse in San Miguel.

The more her family migrated, the more they became exposed to non-Indigenous communities, and it became more difficult for them to use both languages given how Indigenous communities would face discrimination and prejudice for the way they look, speak, and live. They are confronted with slurs and taunts often referred to as "Guajiros" or "Esos oaxaquitas." They begin to repress their Indigenous language in fear of being laughed at and at times attacked. My mother remembers her grandfather 's words to my Nana: "No le hables mixteco, ¿que no ves que aquí hablan puro español la gente? ¿Qué no sabes español?" I can't say for sure, but it seems my Abuelito Luis wanted to repress as much of their Mixtec identity as possible. If Indigenous communities were viewed as inferior and under civilized, he did not want to associate himself with that. He made it an effort for others to know he spoke Spanish. He pushed my Nana to only speak Spanish to her children which she adhered to and as a result my mom is the only one of her 11 siblings who speaks Mixteco. My grandparents stopped speaking Mixteco to their younger children as they moved away from El Pueblo. With my great-grandfather telling them to use Spanish alongside the various forms of discrimination they faced, little by little, my mother's side of the family became a solely Spanish-speaking household.

Yet, despite the change in language, the need for reading and writing continued to be nonexistent for many years. My mother shares her decision to practice non-literacy in that prior to attending church she almost never read or wrote. In her own words, she didn't have an interest in it: "Dice uno, '¿Qué voy a escribir?' Cartas escribía yo hace muchos años, cuando el 92, cuando vine sola, escribía yo cartas para mi mamá o para ustedes cuando se quedaron allá, pero hasta ahí nomás" (Ortega Solano). Here, we see writing used as a tool for communication. Just like my father uses literacy to write letters to my Abuelita, my mother writes (in Spanish) to my Nana to say hello and also to check on her children she's left behind in my Nana's care. Besides that, she has no other purpose or reason for writing. She asks herself, What am I going to write? Why am I going to write? Simply put, it didn't seem important or necessary to her at the time. What mattered to her in 1992 was to work and write to my Nana to see how we were doing. Other than that, her focus was on making sure they were saving money to eventually bring all of us to the US.

Changes in Community Knowledge and Literacy

By 1978, farmworkers from San Miguel started migrating to Fresno, Selma, and Madera in the San Joaquin Central Valley. They begin telling stories of the Central Valley and sharing the benefits of settling in this area—there is a lot of farm work with a great need for workers, and given its distance from the border, a little less visits from La Migra. In a time when personal phones are almost non-existent and letter-writing is only available to literate individuals, storytelling is how knowledge is created and shared. One paisano, after making it to the Central Valley, goes back to San Miguel and shares with the community the kind of work and life possible there. This then motivates others from El Pueblo to come to the Valley. And in the late 1970s, one such story reaches my father, and he begins to make his way to Stockton, in Northern California. It just so happens he has not been able to locate his brother Emiliano whom he knows is in California. His goal then becomes to find his brother and then make their way back to the Central Valley to settle and work there. He eventually finds him working on a cucumber farm in Stockton where he too is able to get work until INS once again shows up at the farm,

> Antes de que llegaran las loncheras, cuando escuchamos ya, pusieron a gritar la gente, 'Córranle porque ahí viene la migra.' Cuando miramos—El pepino no tapa nada, está tendido en el suelo. Ya venía la patrulla para allá, venía para acá y una avioneta arriba. Ahí estábamos corre y corre y la migración detrás de nosotros. No, uno solo de migración nos agarró a los dos, porque íbamos juntos nosotros. Yo y mi hermano corriendo, un mano agarró así aquí, el mío, y otro agarró a tu tío así lo agarró. Ya de ahí nos subieron a una patrulla. (Remigio Luna)

The story my father shares with me is one he's already shared with others. In fact, as soon as someone sees La Migra in the fields, it is their duty to alert everyone else by shouting "Córranle porque ahí viene la migra!" No matter where one may end up, they take these stories with them to be shared amongst their paisanos. They share the good and the bad including places to live, places to work, how to get away from La Migra, which mayordomos to trust and get work from, and even the stores to shop at. Community knowledge is thus spread via storytelling. In practicing non-literacy they place a higher value on verbal communication, storytelling, music, and other practices. The 10-12 hours of their day (6-7 days a week) spent in a non-literate setting plays a vital role in keeping them alive and connected to their communities. Outside of work, their lives are centered on family rearing and community building.

When I think of literacy and non-literacy I like to think of the storytelling and orality that has guided El Pueblo for many years. I imagine how it must have been to be a young person in El Pueblo hearing stories from returning migrants about the richness and beauty of El Norte/El Otro Lado. These stories were told with such emotion, detail, and hope that it instantly persuaded many young men to pack their things and make the dangerous and treacherous journey al Norte. Eventually, these stories became so powerful they convinced entire families like mine to take their young children with them; even pregnant women took the risk and migrated alongside their husbands. All of this done to experience for themselves a new life in El Norte. For El Pueblo, its orality and community storytelling is what pushed migration to where we are today and is an example of the ways this movement has transformed literacy, non-literacy, and knowledge in this community.

Conclusion—Reimagining Community Literacy

In reflecting on my parents' communication and language practices, I wanted to know more about how they make sense of the world around them. How do oral communities interact and communicate with the world around them, especially when living away from home? I wanted to know what they use outside of reading and writing to communicate with others and how others communicate with them. Because I grew up in the US and started school at the age of 5, reading and writing are an important part of my life today. Even as I write this article, I am using words to make sense of the stories my parents told me. I read and write about literacy. I have been in school for the past 26 years and value reading and writing because it allows me to communicate with others and also to gain knowledge from them. However, the more I immerse myself in my parents' world and culture, I come to see the importance of making a distinction between literacy and non-literacy. The purpose of this is not to say one is better than the other, but rather to see how they interact with one other and what we can learn from such interactions. As previously mentioned, with colonialism, literacy was used to conquer Indigenous communities; it was a tool for discrimination and oppression. Today, when looking at the orality of the Mixtec and other Indigenous communities in the US, we can label these as examples of literacy, or we can simply *choose* to acknowledge these as valid forms of communication and community practices and agree that non-literacy is only problematic when defined as a lack of literacy or if viewed through a Western definition of literacy.

Conclusively, while at this point it may not be entirely clear the extent of my parents' deliberate choice to practice literacy as opposed to non-literacy, their stories highlight the frictions shaping migrant lives along these two poles. Moving forward, I hope to conduct more research to develop better methods for understanding the structural forces that support or hinder migrants from choosing one or the other across borders, jobs, communities, and other contexts.

Works Cited

Brandt, Deborah. *Literacy in American Lives.* Cambridge University Press, 2001.

—. "Sponsors of Literacy." *Literacies: A Critical Sourcebook*, edited by Ellen Cushman et al., Bedford/Saint Martin's, 2020, pp. 567-596.

Cifuentes, Bárbara. *Letras sobre voces: Multilingüismo a través de la historia.* CIESAS-INI México, 1998.

De Genova, Nicholas P. "Migrant 'Illegality' and Deportability in Everyday Life." *Annual Review of Anthropology*, vol. 31, no. 1, 2002, pp. 419-447. doi:10.1146/annurev.anthro.31.040402.085432.

Garcia Canclini, Nestor. *Culturas Híbridas: Estrategias para Entrar y Salir de la Modernidad.* Debolsillo, 1995.

Gilmore, Perry and Leisy Wyman. "An Ethnographic Long Look: Language and Literacy Over Time and Space in Alaska Native Communities." *Literacies: A Critical Sourcebook*, edited by Ellen Cushman et al., Bedford/St Martin's, 2020, pp. 121-138.

Goody, Jack, and Ian Watt. "The Consequences of Literacy." *Comparative Studies in Society and History*, vol. 5, no. 3, 1962, pp. 304-345.

Hernandez-Zamora, Gregorio. *Decolonizing Literacy: Mexican Lives in the Era of Global Capitalism*, Channel View Publications, 2010.

Horton, Sarah B. "Ghost workers: The Implications of Governing Immigration Through Crime for Migrant Workplaces." *Anthropology of Work Review*, vol. 37, no. 1, 2016, pp. 11-23. https://doi.org/10.1111/awr.12081.

—. "Identity Loan: The Moral Economy of Migrant Document Exchange in California's Central Valley." *Journal of the American Ethnological Society*, vol. 42, no. 1, 2015, pp. 55-67. https://doi.org/10.1111/amet.12115.

Jackson, Rachel C., and Dorothy W. DeLaune. "Decolonizing Community Writing with Community Listening: Story, Transrhetorical Resistance, and Indigenous-Cultural Literacy Activism." *Community Literacy Journal*, vol. 13, no.1, 2018, pp. 37–54. doi:10.1353/clj.2018.0020.

Kalmar, Tomás M. *Illegal Alphabets and Adult Biliteracy.* Routledge, 2015.

King, Linda. *Roots of Identity: Language and Literacy in Mexico.* Stanford University Press, 1994.

Lyons, Scott R. "Rhetorical Sovereignty: What do American Indians Want From writing?" *College Composition and Communication*, vol. 51, no. 3, 2000, pp. 447-468. doi:10.2307/35874.

—. "There's No Translation for It: The Rhetorical Sovereignty of IndigenousLanguages." *Cross-Language Relations in Composition*, edited by Bruce Horner et al., Southern Illinois University Press, 2014, pp. 127–141.

Ortega Solano, Josefina. Personal interview. 20 May 2022.

Powell, Malea. "Rhetorics of Survivance: How American Indians Use Writing." *College Composition and Communication*, vol. 53, no. 2, 2002, pp. 396-434. http://www.jstor.org/stable/1512132.

Purcell-Gates, Victoria. "Literacy Worlds of Children of Migrant Farmworker Communities Participating in a Migrant Head Start Program." *Research in the Teaching of English*, vol. 48, no. 1, 2013, pp. 68-97. https://www.jstor.org/stable/24398647.

Remigio Luna, Policarpo P. Personal interview. 20 May 2022.

Ribero, Ana M. "Citizenship." *Decolonizing Rhetoric and Composition Studies: New Latinx Keywords for Theory and Pedagogy*, edited by Iris D. Ruiz and Raul Sanchez, Palgrave Macmillan, 2016, pp. 31-45.

Rios. Gabriela R. "Cultivating Indigenousland-based literacies and rhetorics." *Literacy in Composition Studies*, vol. 3, no. 1, 2015, pp. 60-70.

—. "Mestizaje." *Decolonizing Rhetoric and Composition Studies: New Latinx Keywords for Theory and Pedagogy*, edited by Iris D. Ruiz and Raul Sanchez, Palgrave Macmillan, 2016, pp. 109-124.

Stephen, Lynn. *Transborder Lives: IndigenousOaxacans in Mexico, California, and Oregon*. Duke University Press, 2007.

Street, Brian. "The Implications of the 'New Literacy Studies' for Literacy Education." *English in Education*, vol. 31, no. 3, 1997, pp. 45-59.

Varsanyi, Monica W. "Documenting Undocumented Migrants: The Matriculas Consulares as Neoliberal Local Membership." *Geopolitics*, vol. 12, no. 2, 2007, pp. 299-319. doi:10.1080/14650040601169014.

Vieira, Kate. *American by Paper: How Documents Matter in Immigrant Literacy*. Minneapolis, University of Minnesota Press, 2016.

Wan, Amy J. "Literacy Training, Americanization, and the Cultivation of the Productive Worker-Citizen." *Producing Good Citizens : Literacy Training in Anxious Times*, edited by David Bartholomae and Jean Ferguson Carr, University of Pittsburgh Press, 2014, pp. 38-71.

Author Bio

Guadalupe Remigio Ortega (she/her) is a PhD candidate at the University of Wisconsin-Madison. Her research focuses on Indigenous(Mixtec) literacies and knowledge, community literacies, oral histories, and border and migrant rhetorics. Her current project is a collection of oral histories and testimonios of Mixtec migrant farmworkers in Fresno, California, whose traditional and non-traditional literacy practices demonstrate the complexities of Mixtec literacies and how these, alongside the intersectionality of Mixtec identity in the United States, challenge current dominant discourses on literacy, illiteracy, and non-literacy. Lupe has eight years of teaching experience including first-year writing (at the university and community college level), intermediate composition, and technical communication for STEM majors. Her teaching pedagogy focuses on creating a student-centered classroom that acknowledges the diverse backgrounds and learning styles of all students.

Finding the Lorde in Me: Using Lordean Counterstory to Thwart Bureaucratic Violence in Community-Based Literacy Projects

Teigha VanHester

Abstract

This autoethnography chronicles an Afro-Polynesian femme scholar's struggle to secure funding for research due to bureaucratic violence and the strategic potential of Lordean counterstorying to write a way free for Black and Brown scholar-activists and community-based projects. Extending the work of previous scholars who discuss counterstory and institutional violence, this work uses re-imagination and creativity to mobilize radical research agendas geared towards empowering and amplifying community-based literacies.

Keywords: auto-ethnography, Black, femme, counterstory, community, community writing, faculty, institutional violence, literacy, Audre Lorde, pleasure activism, radical imagination, research, research agenda, tenure-track

On an oppressively hot August afternoon, I put the finishing touches on my new office. I made sure my wrestling figurines of MJF, Adam Cole, and CM Punk were devoid of dust or any imperfections, alphabetized and categorized books, positioned LEGO skylines of Paris and Shanghai, and then collapsed into a $40 midcentury modern loveseat I found at an indie grocery store with my department chair. Gazing around, my office walls were covered in art, concert posters, and pictures of my nephew, Maxton, and plant stands fanning out lush green foliage in every direction. Sure, I could have been prepping for the courses I was to teach in the coming week or feverishly attending Faculty Welcome Week sessions, but I knew that putting my stamp on this place mattered. I wanted my colleagues, administrators, and students to know that I was here, this was my new homeplace, cultivated in love, kitsch, and my truth.

I had/have no interest in accumulating academic clout or power, I don't play politics; instead, I have what has been described as performing an "unbossed and unbothered" Chisholm-esque energy. I am driven as a scholar-activist to challenge the status quo, resist limitations, fight with precision and purpose, and demand a reimagination of the co-opted academy. Make no mistake, this is labor, undervalued and often not compensated but essential to an ethos steeped in liberation and sovereignty. So, in my new office, adorned from corner to corner with my contradictory, unique, sarcastic flair, I took a deep breath, smiled, and set out to not only survive the tenure-track but thrive within it.

Those first weeks and months of the semester were a whirlwind. Being able to navigate obstacles, violence, committee invitations, disciplinary-specific webinars, department meetings, student crises, and the illusive beast that is research required community, solidarity, and intellectual ancestry. Scholar-activists often pursue academia for the opportunity to conduct research and write scholarship (at least I hope I am not alone in this). I wanted my research to align with the need for the academy to radically reassess what research is and how it is done in the 21st century. A view of research that allowed podcast series, non-academic publications, artistic collections, social media content creation, public archival and community-engaged projects to be seen as the scholarship they are. I saw amazing work from senior-level colleagues, but as a first-year professor, I didn't see how without youthful naivety (or job security) I would be able to advance a non-traditional research agenda that required institutional support, external funding, and publications that adhered to tenure-track guidelines calling for peer-reviewed articles or book publications as the only scholarly pursuits worthy of our time. To see my research validated, funded, and published, I had to step into the unknown, take a risk, and write a way free.

The goal of this article is to equip scholar-activists with a key concept for thwarting institutional violence that targets our radical research agendas or our emphasis on community writing and literacies that I call Lordean Counterstorying. By using the gospel of the warrior poet Audre Lorde's writings on anger, love, and silence as key for resistance, this article seeks to present Lordean counterstorying as a strategy for surviving and thriving in our scholastic truth when faced with institutional violence to radically reimagine research and scholarship needs. Institutional violence is not only felt in the academy, but it can be felt in spaces where community literacy projects seek funding and support for their initiatives as well. Aligning with Black Feminist Scholarship, this work blends lived experience with critical implications to aid in the development of a strategic action plan or the building of a community necessary to complete our exigent work, specifically securing the necessary funding. Lordean counterstorying is an embodied and compositional response that challenges institutional violence and neoliberal narratives by repurposing anger, eros (love), and language in ways that allow for radical reimagining of scholar-activists' positionality. As a tool, Lordean counterstorying advances scholar-activist resilience, flexibility, and authenticity. This is especially useful for junior faculty and/or emerging community-based intellectuals.

The chances of securing any significant amount of research funding as a first-year assistant professor, fellow, lecturer, contingent faculty, or community organizer feels as likely as finding a Serena Williams-like pickleball partner. But no matter how unlikely the opportunity, I argue we should still be prepared. The story that follows is my own quest to fund my research agenda through competing for an equipment fund grant sponsored by my private PWI. I do not think that my story is necessarily oozing with drama and surprises, but I do know it is important to share, especially with those engaged in community writing and research because we are inherently inundated by our neoliberal institutional narratives to undervalue ourselves and our research. Whether those narratives are attempting to invoke humility, honesty, or fear in Black and Brown scholar-activists, I am not here to speculate. I am here to say, though, that we (as individuals, communities, and scholars) have every right to demand more and fight for more. Our work is not a pursuit in vanity, but it is a compulsion to show our communities' truth and inherent value.

This autoethnographic-adjacent piece speaks directly to my experience. I invite my fellow community writing scholar-activist kinfolk to find their truth within Lorde's work and the radical, resistance potential of counterstorying. Throughout this paper, I will focus on how this embodied and compositional strategy works to support the importance of community-based research. In her 2017 CCW keynote address, Ellen Cushman states, "community-based research ... becomes a microcosm for the learning ecologies and networks we hope to inspire, especially in this time of great division, uncertainty, and cultivation of fear of others" (18). We need our community-based research and teaching to be validated, compensated, and supported now more than ever. The effects of critical community research and writing being marginalized and undervalued is one of many intersections that contribute to books being banned, bodily autonomy being reversed, and genocide being justified. As community-based scholar-activists, our work does a myriad of things—it can humanize, illuminate, story, celebrate, and speak truth to power—but it most importantly works to inspire, develop peace/justice, and place harmony into praxis. The concept of Lordean counterstorying as strategy in community-based writing is my attempt to heed Cushman's call, to inspire possibilities and counterattacks to neoliberal violence coming in the form of devaluation of community-based labor, programs, and projects.

The Key Tenets of Lordean Counterstory

Lordean counterstorying is a strategy for radical resistance and reclamation that juxtaposes the work of Audre Lorde and the method of counterstory to illuminate sustainable strategies of resistance and research for all levels of scholars, activists, and/or community-based practitioners. Lordean counterstory as a method (both embodied practice and literary genre) has the potential context and opportunity to make sense of a community-based scholar-activist's positionality, identity, and mission within the academy and/or community organizing. It calls for the transformation of the love (erotic), anger, and silence into motivating forces that can be used to combat the invalidation of our communities, work, and literacies. Lorde's arguably most famous piece "The Master's Tools will not Dismantle the Master's House" highlights the need for us to identify imaginative ways of sustaining our work, lives, and teaching in the face of ever present—and at times all consuming—violence.

As defined by Aja Martinez, "[c]ounterstory [is] a method for telling stories by people whose experiences are not often told. Counterstory as methodology serves to expose, analyze, and challenge stock stories of racial privilege and can help to strengthen traditions of social, political, and cultural survival and resistance" (34). As a rhetorical method, counterstory provides the field of RhetComp a tangible way to employ CRT in scholarship and pedagogy. Community-based researchers can utilize

CRT counterstory to reclaim their identity and lived experience and provide (alternative) narratives and histories in the making (Toliver 509). In essence, counterstory expands the narratives available to us across the humanities, performances, and rhetoric in ways that challenge hegemonic, heteronormative dominance in credibility, validity, and visibility. Audre Lorde as a scholar and warrior poet embodied the essence of everything she published. Her words radically articulated approaches for sustainable resistance, eloquently challenged dominant narratives of oppression, and unapologetically centered Black Women's emotive intellect in ways that continue to inform movements today. Lordean counterstory as a strategy then situates the intellectual legacy of Lorde—her embodied praxis and effortless prose—regarding anger and eros with CRT counterstory to create an opportunity for relentless advocacy for scholar-activism based in and with community. For community-based scholar-activists, Lordean counterstorying (as opposed to CRT counterstorying) utilizes Lorde's intellectual ancestry to challenge dominant narratives and to curtail instances where community-based work is subjected to various forms of institutional violence. Lordean counterstory as a strategy also does the very important work of validating and celebrating community-based scholar-activists' critical, full, authentic humanity—guided by our commitment to empathy and compassion. As an embodied and compositional concept, Lordean counterstory inspires scholar-activists to honor the emotions of anger and eros (love) in projects, initiatives, and research, allowing us to see them not as signs of weakness, fragility, or vulnerability. Instead, community-based scholar-activists' ability to experience anger and eros signal authenticity, ferocity, and passion. With Lordean counterstory, scholar-activists can begin to develop ways of writing radical resistance, channeling unapologetic passion, and embodying dissent.

Letting Love Lead: Counterstorying Lordean Eros

> *"Our erotic knowledge empowers us, becomes a lens through which we scrutinize all aspects of our existence, forcing us to evaluate those aspects honestly in terms of their relative meaning in our lives."*
>
> —Audre Lorde

The journey of any scholar-activist's identity or community literacy project starts with an agenda. Articulating my research agenda is something that I constantly struggled with as I inched towards my dissertation defense. In a mock interview I did while on the market with my dissertation committee, I vividly remember Dr. Ela Przybylo gently suggested that I embellish my plan, even if I know the trajectory may change. I knew my dedication to researching things that brought love, joy, and liberty for myself and my communities was considered radical for scholars outside of Race, Women's, Gender, Sexuality Studies or Cultural Rhetoric departments. As a self-defined Afro-Polynesian femme scholar, I can tell when I walk into a room, raise my hand in a meeting, or am featured on a conference abstract, that some people expect my research to come from a place of anger at societal injustices and oppressions. I refused to allow oversimplified typecasting to define me or my work, just as it should not define my community. Thus, while on the market, I was fully transparent about the need for research to be sustained in joy, adventure, and healing—something radical to life-long academics indoctrinated into the neoliberal narrative. We begin writing our Lordean counterstory in our research agenda by centering love and the galvanizing force of its power to inspire us.

In "Uses of the Erotic: The Erotic as Power," Lorde charts the etymology of the term eros, which means to love; and yet, society relinquishes erotic love to the bedroom, when its potential should extend far beyond the private. As emerging scholars in community-based research, it is imperative to center love and pleasure in our research. Our passion for the work will free us from the sort of sentiment eloquently discussed in adrienne maree brown's collection *Pleasure Activism: The Politics of Feeling Good*. When selecting a research area, when radically reimagined, when steeping community-based projects in literacies of love—one can feel as though their research is indulgent, self-serving, or lacks exigency (brown 17). Lordean counterstorying and its key tenet in creating eros (love) directly challenges that and speaks to the violent narratives that call the pursuit of love and passion in academia or social justice community work a non-scholastic pursuit, unimportant, or vain (Redden 2018). Not only is the idea that love is not worthy of research, funding, or validation incorrect, it is one of the ways in which institutional violence is perpetrated. To combat that violence, we need to remember the words of Ersula Ore, Kim Weiser, and Christina Cedillo: "so long as mainstream education continues to be *whitestream* education, the academy will continue to demean and exclude our culturally situated knowledge-making processes, our use of language, our bodymindspirits, and the stories we tell, including our research" (207). If Lorde challenges us to center love and institutional violence devalues our cultural creations (borne of love and in community), using Lordean counterstorying allows us to shift our view of our scholar-activist self from a deficiency lens (that of institutional violence) to a lens of abundance (Lordean eros).

Being at odds with our trueness, aliveness, leads to an existence where violence is not only placed upon us, but also lives within us (brown 6). It also perpetuates a world within which we have no interest (hopefully) in occupying. So, while "we have been raised to fear the *yes* within ourselves, our deepest cravings" (Lorde 57), we also have the opportunity, in defining and cultivating our research agenda, to do the work that we *need*. When we love our work, when we choose to survive and thrive in spite of violence, we create theory, concepts, movements, projects that are built in the love of Lordean counterstory and are also akin to the liberatory strategies of hooks who stated, "when we hold fast to our beliefs… folks will yearn, yes yearn, to be a part of [our movement]" (11). The energy we perform when talking about our work, passions, projects, and people is contagious. By loving fully, we challenge others to do the same and radically reimagine the power of love, a charge given to us in the use of Lordean eros and counterstorying research agendas.

I painstakingly negotiated, rewrote, revised, remixed, deleted, and amended a cacophony of research trajectories and strategies that had to (1) be authentic, (2) bring joy, (3) explore potential, (4) place Black and Brown liberation into praxis, (5) heal, and (6) be sustainable. Something that took me a while to understand as I engaged in this thought work was that my research had to embody the qualities listed above for my communities and for myself. Then like a lightning bolt, I was reminded of Treva Lindsey's words that I paraphrased in my notebook during one of her lectures: our work exists and is most meaningful when rage and joy are experienced simultaneously (2023). So, with this priceless nugget of intellectual ancestry squirreled away in my mind, I began to devise a plan—a plan that would help me achieve tenure, help expand the potential for Afro-Polynesian liberation, empower my community, and build spaces of fun, sovereignty, play, and authenticity along the way.

Scholars such as Jafari Allen, Lyndon Gill, Alexis Pauline Gumbs, and Ela Przybylo and Kaiya Jacobs situate Lorde's work regarding eros and the erotics within a queer theory lens to highlight the importance of abundance, truth, and authenticity in queer worldmaking, embodiment, and performance. The use of Lordean erotics has led to advancements in the understanding of the erotic, from the term eros as love, desire, pleasure; not always to be seen as private, deviant shameful behavior, but more fluid and complex. According to Jafari Allen, "[A] Lordean Eros [is] pleasure in coming to know what we know about ourselves and our world (epistemological pleasure) and pleasure in teaching what we have learned and learning from those who find pleasure in teaching us (pedagogical pleasure)" (14). Through this redefinition of the erotic, scholars, activists, and communities can center the importance of pleasure and passion in their work, solidarity, and activism.

Putting Lordean Love-Lead Research into Praxis

The community literacies my research agenda was working to empower, center, and uplift sought to provide young Black and Brown scholar-activists (Butler students and (in the future) Indianapolis-area scholar-activists) with communal literacies for healing, leisure, rest, and resistance. Historically, Black and Brown bodies have been validated and valued largely in terms of the labor they provide in the advancement of capitalism and white supremacy. I align my community-based research agenda with scholar-activists like Tricia Hersey of the Nap Ministries, adrienne maree brown's call for pleasure activism, and the power of Lorde's discussions on the erotic, anger, and transformation of silence into action. I believe that communal literacies and the work we do in and with the community starts from a subjective, culturally-situated approach to advancing literacies of healing, mindfulness, and sovereign embodiment.

Some communities may have already completed this work, but I could see at my PWI that many of our Black and Brown students were compelled to excel, assimilate, and silence their intersectionality in exchange for access to institutions that equate worth to capitalist achievement. Using Lordean counterstorying strategies, I wanted to challenge that narrative and join the myriad of scholar-activists whose research advances the notion that Black and Brown bodies are worthy of rest, love, pleasure, and joy. Thus, it was serendipitous during this research epiphany to see the CfP for the "Equipment Fund" on my Daily Digest listserv for my institution. The requirements were relatively straightforward—can't be used for space, must relate to faculty research, priority given to student-involved research, and half of equipment needs to be covered by faculty college. The leanings to equipment required for STEM-fields was inherent, but I wanted to empower others in the Humanities and Social Sciences to see the radical potential of our community-based research.

So, with the full support of my amazing chair, I wrote a proposal to purchase a meditation pod for emerging Black and Brown scholar-activists (students) within the College of Liberal Arts and Sciences. This research aligned with my agenda to discover ways to situate healing and love our research. It would allow students to place into praxis mindfulness and healing from any potential microaggressions or stressors they may experience in earlier classes by providing a space for privacy, recentering, and rest. It was my hypothesis that with this pod, students of color would see that the institution acknowledged the struggles they might be facing in the day to day and support marginalized students with the hopes of increasing student attendance, resilience, and prioritizing wellness practices into their lifestyle. We would have been the first higher education institution to acquire a meditation pod and this initiative could serve as a strategy for setting my home institution apart from other benchmark institutions while simultaneously empowering Black and Brown students to prioritize their mental health and academic success in the face of insurmountable adversity. For the pilot, the students selected to have access to the pods would be paid to rest and engage in a series of interviews with me about their experiences with the pod and in their classes to improve the collegiate experience of our most vulnerable student populations. Lordean counterstorying illuminated the potential for loving this community of student scholar-activists by imagining a place where they can practice self-love and self-care, strategies that would galvanize them to understand its significance and situate it within their personal and professional lives.

Black and Brown students at a PWI can experience the same imposter syndrome in their classes as felt by Black and Brown community scholar-activists in their research. Through the meditation pod project, my goal was to empower our marginalized students to prioritize, cultivate, and embody literacies for self-care, self-love, healing, and rest as key to their success in the public sphere. I agree with the concept of literacy as defined by the *CLJ* website: "the realm where attention is paid not just to content or to knowledge but to the symbolic means by which it is represented and used. Thus, literacy makes reference not just to letters and to text but to other multimodal, technological, and embodied representations, as well." Using that definition and maintaining a connection with Lordean counterstory, I felt as though this project situated embodied literacies of meditation, breathwork, and mindfulness as a potentially transformational loving strategy for Black and Brown students' survival, joy, and academic success in a PWI. Practicing mindfulness, experiencing a reprieve from surveillance, and having a private space for 15-30 minutes where students could breathe, reset, and persist in their courses (I hypothesized) would provide the opportunity for Black and Brown student bodies (literally) to see themselves not as subjects only valued based on their output – understanding themselves to be valued subjects based on their input, capable of prioritizing their own mental health.

The project proposal invigorated me. With so many of our institutions "prioritizing" DEI initiatives, I felt as though it would be difficult to challenge such an innovative and (dare I say) radical proposal. I was rewriting the equipment fund, I was meeting the needs of my research agenda, and I was engaging in a project that my department and I thought could transform underrepresented student support in revolutionary ways. During finals week of my first full semester as an assistant professor, I received an email congratulating me on receiving the equipment fund grant. Little did I know that although a counterstory of Lordean eros got me here, it would take so much more to navigate the looming neoliberal minefield I was about to traverse.

Speak Truth To Power: Counterstorying with Lordean Language

> *"For we have been socialized to respect fear more than our own needs for language and definition, and while we wait in the silence for that final luxury of fearlessness, the weight of that silence will choke us."*
>
> —Audre Lorde

Institutional violence, as referred to throughout this work, is interrogated heavily by the work of other community literacy scholars and cultural rhetoric scholars who discuss the violence marginalized/underrepresented subjects experience in the academy, society, and in neoliberal institutions. Institutional violence may not be overt, but it follows a 'business as usual' form of violence that, according to Ore et al., "[D]raw attention to the academy's complicity—indeed, centrality—in promoting the oppressive structures and dominant culture's imaginary that continue to harm [Black folx]" ("Diversity is not Enough" 207). These violent acts are not specific to my institution; they can be seen throughout the academy where marginalized/underrepresented scholars are expected to speak their truth, translate that truth into the dominant format, and sacrifice time, resources, and research to meet the requirements of arbitrary structures with the ability to affect our employability (Ore et al. "Diversity is not Enough" 208). And it is important to remember that institutional violence is meant to only encumber those in the margins. As Victor Del Hierro and colleagues remind us, "Works on the margins are never meant to expand the center; in naming something or someone marginal we are reiterating and confirming their place in the relationship. Within academia and outside of it, we encounter examples of how marginalization operates as a colonizing tool to make one believe that a static center exists" (Del Hierro et al. 2016). The violence one can experience at an institution that leans towards neo-liberal narratives is complex. I feel comfortable writing this article and speaking to this experience not only because it is my truth, but also because I refuse to single out any one person, group, department, or entity as the culprit for my forthcoming struggles. It is systemic and takes many forms.

After being awarded the equipment funds, I began to distribute and celebrate the coming project internally and externally. As with any research project, I had identified a variety of places to publish the work, informed colleagues in department meetings, and began the IRB process for the student participants. I was excited and ready to bring about a project that could improve the marginalized student community experience at my institution when the project, the Race, Gender, and Sexuality Studies (RGSS) program steering committee, and I unearthed the ever-present roadblocks and bureaucratic nonsense (for lack of a better term) that would descend upon us.

It began with concerns about a location for the pod, then there was an error on the application that required the matching funding to come from the department and not the overall College of Liberal Arts and Sciences, and lastly a wild card concern about accessibility. For months, my chair and I sent emails, sat through meetings, and held strategy sessions over coffee at least once a week to refute concerns. It was mayhem. So many times, I wanted to quit, forget the project, and restructure my research agenda, but my program director would not allow it. Her energy—as a veteran of the institution's culture, literacy, and battle strategy—empowered me to continue fighting for the project. She called in favors, met with deans, highlighted flaws in documents, toured the building with facilities, and at times held more firmly to the need for this work than I.

Just as Lordean counterstorying with eros aided in navigating the work of identifying my research agenda and was key in thwarting institutional violence performed via myths of the inferiority of love-based community research, the planning phase required skills to traverse a process plagued by institutional violence. As soon as the funds were awarded to secure the pod, the neoliberal institution shifted its support to bureaucratic violence in the form of complex reporting requirements, institutional red tape, and institutional policies that only live in the memory of those with 20-plus years of engagement with the institution. This is how institutional violence manifests and perpetuates epistemic exclusion, "a form of scholarly delegitimization rooted in disciplinary biases about what types of research are valued as well as social identity-based biases against individuals from marginalized groups … [that] may have a disproportionately negative effect on women and faculty of color due to negative stereotypes about their competence, and their likelihood of engaging in research outside of the disciplinary mainstream" (Settles et al. 32). Without the proper strategy, dissent, and support, community-based research and researchers suffer.

Acknowledging the need for support—vocalized, lived, and steeped in solidarity—was essential. We tag teamed this with the ferocity of Darby Allen and Sting (I really enjoy wrestling): when I needed a break, my program director stepped up; when she got stumped, I suggested solutions; and so it went for months, but I learned I wasn't alone, and I learned I didn't have to settle. Community-based research allows us to engage with various communities in the world, but community-based researchers must remember the importance of community in the academy and ask for it. Now depending on one's institution, available colleagues, and institutional climate, this may not be simple, but it is not impossible. Inviting solidarity from established scholar-activists in the communities we love and work to liberate is as essential as junior and emerging scholar-activists who inarguably need mentorship, guidance, institutional literacies, and accomplice-ship.

Creating a Way: Counterstorying with Lordean Anger

> *"[T]he strength of women lies in recognizing differences between us as creative, and in standing to those distortions which we inherited without blame, but which are now ours to alter. The angers of women can transform difference through insight into power. For anger between peers births change, not destruction, and the discomfort and sense of loss it often causes is not fatal, but a sign of growth."*
>
> —Audre Lorde

Lordean anger is directly drawn from the speech "The Use of Anger: Women Responding to Racism" in which Lorde speaks of the daily micro- and macro- aggressions faced by Black Women in feminist spaces and movements (127). While acknowledging the ineffectiveness of hate, guilt, and silence, Lorde challenges the white women in the audience to understand how they contribute to racist practices, while claiming to be allies and feminists. She also, more implicitly, speaks to Black Women, making visible the ways they can and do use their anger creatively as a driving force for their liberation and response to the matrices of domination, within which their identities are deemed irrelevant. Lorde informed the audience in her talk that, "Every woman has a well-stocked arsenal of anger potentially useful against those oppressions, personal and institutional, which brought that anger into being" (144). Lorde challenges us to see anger as utilized with precision, intent, and strategy as an emotion that can lead to survival, solidarity, sisterhood, and change.

After months of fighting and meeting and indecision, my RGSS kinfolk and I were angry and exhausted. There were no more emails to send, no more time for half answers, no more patience for the myriad of emerging stakeholders that we were tasked with lobbying to our cause. Institutional violence pretends that it operates in coincidences, bureaucratic processes, and without bias, but it is that non-acknowledgement and lack of accountability and transparency that is the most violent of them all. In these moments it is very easy to want to release "hood Teyoncé" to the masses, but I know that would only prove them right. I would have to control my emotive state, not silence it but intentionally channel that anger and frustration into motivation. It became clear: we had to develop a new course of action, a Plan B. The plan became to secure the equipment funds at all costs. I scheduled a meeting with the dean of our college with the goals of getting a definitive answer on the meditation pod and having a comprehensive plan to pivot the funds and research to something that still aligned with my desire to work in the borderlands of Black and Brown rage and joy in a way that was impactful and sustainable.

Sometimes regardless of the research agendas/projects, we are forced to adapt—at least temporarily. I spent weeks thinking about a different project that would require funds for equipment that cultivated the same excitement as the meditation pods. I was consumed by the anger I felt towards the bureaucratic violence I had endured. If I am being completely honest, I wanted to just go back into my gorgeous office, pump out some standard archival research, get tenure, and settle for status quo mediocrity. But being raised by the best single mother in South Central Los Angeles who raised me to know my default setting was unapologetic and authentic excellence, I knew the perfect Teigha-esque research project and agenda inhabited the recesses of my brain. I was reminded of a "coming to Jesus" moment I had when reading SA Smythe's "Can I Get a Witness? Black Feminism, Trans Embodiment, and Thriving Past the Fault Lines of Care" inviting Black Feminists "to continue living into their principles by sitting with the discomfort and then operationalizing that feeling to struggle and shift from oppressive tendencies and structures" (104). As marginalized members in society and the academy, scholar-activists must (a) live their truth, (b) feel fully, and (c) make use of the elements and interactions provided to them.

Everything has a purpose and can provide energy to the work of the Black, queer femme scholar. Repurposing anger, just like repurposing food waste or seeds, inevitably leads to sustainable growth. Marginalized folks can harvest that anger in transformative ways of meaning-making, allowing that anger to nourish and give life to creativity. This sentiment is echoed in the work of Jonathan Alexander and Jacqueline Rhodes, who tell us that composing queerness is an impossible task due to the ambiguity therein where the emotions one feels and attempts to compose are ones we "do not always know what to do with or know how to contain" (197). With identities steeped in the perpetual act of becoming, the perpetual act of being affected and called to a position of hypervisibility or invisibility, the Black, queer femme scholar-activist and scholar-creative benefits from authenticity and, as Tommaso Milan discusses, an approach to queer composing of the self that resists the "facile" adoptions of queer identities and emotion-based composing (444).

Neoliberalism does not allow imagination and experimentation; instead, it relies on the traditional status quo that dictates its next move based on benchmark organizational success, making others take the risk at the cost of their own right to innovation. For us in community literacy work, we know the personal is political, we know that it is through our own liberation that we can liberate others, and so I went back to reflect on my community and myself as a beautiful cacophony of potential. We knew the 'no' was coming, but *they* didn't know I was working on a plan.

Using Lordean anger, I refused to allow my rage to end in surrender, I creatively used that anger to shift my project to another that did not pose the same problems as they claimed came about in the initial project. I used Lordean eros to think about other ways of liberating my community akin to the overarching goals of healing, rest, love, and joy. I did this by looking at what I love and would want to share with others. Lordean counterstorying not only provides a new way of articulating the needs of our community, writing our research, and requests for funding, but it is also a strategy that can be used in our thought work or radical reimagining that galvanizes us with the ability to shift and reorient in the face of adversity. As scholar-activists, we have multiple projects in our minds or notebooks. I remember my dissertation chair suggesting I put ideas that emerge in my dissertation work on a post-it for another project. I was inundated with post-it notes.

In the next meeting, we got the no. We got some push back about the same logistical, bureaucratic violence we had grown accustomed to over the course of this saga. In response, I presented an alternative plan. My alternative plan came from my post-it notes and strategic reflection. As a Black, Fijian, American Samoan, Irish femme intellectual, that plan centered round researching in the water. Every corner of my identity centers around the water—my ancestors crossed it, I lived my childhood years in it, and so much of my healing practices require engagement with it. I realized that diasporic (Black and Polynesian) histories, cultures, and identities are not in traditional archives but are present in what I call sunken archives. So much of who we are, our legacy, our connections, our desires are buried in the world's two largest oceans. I proposed an alternative plan that would allow me to further research this Black and Brown communal connection to the water—as a site of healing, history, and home. The ocean for Black and Brown people is a site of anger, love, and healing that inextricably links to the words of Audre Lorde and the need to radically reimagine the potential spaces and places where Humanities and Social Science research can be conducted. Armed with the intellectual ancestry of Alexis Pauline Gumbs' *Undrowned: Black Feminist Lessons from Marine Animals* and *Dub: Finding Ceremony*, the works of Jamaica Kincaid, Saidiya Hartman's *Lose Your Mother*, and the Merwomanist Jalondra Davis, we made the case.

I am not sure if it was the guilt of not being able to support the meditation pod, actual intrigue in the new project proposal, excitement that other funding for this project had been attained, or an understanding that this project is something that the college could get behind, but the dean endorsed the updated project and I was able to use the equipment funds for the SCUBA and AV equipment I would need to move forward with my work. As we left the meeting, we were invigorated and so excited to have this victory. In the summer of 2023, I went to Aotearoa (also known as New Zealand) and began my new research project that focused on theorizing the potential of aquatic literacies in Afro-Polynesian kinkeeping, community healing, and ancestry. Conducting sunken archival research requires physically diving into the ruins of transatlantic slave ships and utilizing key tenets of Maori/Oceania Feminist resistance and liberation, I am theorizing that the connecting, healing, and loving practices that members of the Black, Polynesian, and Afro-Polynesian community utilize to heal from the harms of capitalism, colonization, and imperialism reveals legacies, knowledges, and connections that are just below the surface, in the still, quiet, ferocious sea. My hope is that this work/project helps members of the Black diaspora (specifically) see the water as a homeplace, to show them an often-forgotten site of our heritage and legacy. Capitalism, colonialism, and imperialism have led to many Black folks fearing the sea, when really the sea was the only place between our native Africa and the Caribbean where we could attempt to preserve our freedom.

It is important to note that while the meditation pod project about Black and Brown healing and consciousness was not going to be approved, I firmly believe it will happen eventually. Currently, I am working with other organizations on and off campus to advance that project. A "no" from institutions, bureaucrats, and neoliberals cannot and will not define our work; our persistence has the power to move forward any initiative that we choose. In this instance, I chose not to dwell on this impending denial but instead to strategize with other stakeholders, spaces, and places where the answer can shift to an enthusiastic "YES!"

Nevertheless, We Persisted

> *"I urge each one of us...to reach down into that deep place of knowledge inside herself and touch that terror and loathing of any difference that lives there. See whose face it wears. Then the personal as the political can begin to illuminate all our choices".*
>
> —Audre Lorde

Black and Brown community-based scholar-activists do not often have the luxury of adhering to a neoliberal understanding of work-life/personal-professional balance (Kelenyi 18). Our survival and ability to thrive are oftentimes intricately interwoven within our subject-position. Often, I have borne witness to the sacrifice of life, to continue the work and the death of the personal in exchange for the professional. Unfortunately, this is an all too often feature of academic violence that remains unchecked.

Only being able to complete research and writing over the summer while not on contract—violence. Inability to incorporate articles/books related to one's research into the classroom—violence. Minimal start-up funds or access to research-related funding in the Humanities—violence. Institutional service requirements that take precedent over community engagement—violence. We must begin to radically reimagine strategies for prioritizing sustainable engagement over bureaucratic deliverables. Community-based research should not be defined by external forces, devoid of fiscal, temporal, or personnel support; instead, it should be defined internally by the researcher and the communities and based on that definition, we should be able to demand support and equity from the external. This work, our work, is a reclamation of "research and professional paths unhindered by white interests" (Ore et al. "Diversity is not justice" 601).

Lordean counterstorying as performed in this article and research project empowered my community-based research to thrive—in love, through language, and with anger. I am aware that my experience may not be available, practical, or applicable to all community-based researchers, but we all have the opportunity to radically reimagine a way forward. Regardless of status, research, or need, we all as community-based researchers have a role to play in supporting work adjacent to our own and developing a network of practitioners committed to empowering community-based research, funding, and job security for one another. Allowing our work, our academic homeplaces, and accomplice-ship to be led in love and liberation is what our work is all about.

Works Cited

Alexander, Jonathan and Jacqueline Rhodes. "Queer: An Impossible Subject for Composition." *JAC*, vol. 31, no. 1-2, 2011, pp. 197.

Allen, Jafari. *¡Venceremos? The Erotics of Self-Making in Cuba.* Duke UP, 2011.

brown, adrienne maree. *Emergent Strategy: Shaping Change, Changing Worlds.* AK Press, 2017.

—. *Pleasure Activism: The Politics of Feeling Good.* AK Press, 2019.

Cushman, Ellen. "2017 Conference on Community Writing Keynote Address: Place and Relationships in Community Writing." *Community Literacy Journal,* vol. 12, no. 2, 2018, pp. 17-26.

Community Literacy Journal. "Home." https://digitalcommons.fiu.edu/communityliteracy/. Accessed 12 November 2023.

Del Hierro, Victor, et al. "We Are Here: Negotiating Difference and Alliance in Spaces of Cultural Rhetorics." *enculturation,* 2016, https://enculturation.net/we-are-here.

Gill, Lyndon. "In the Realm of Our Lorde: Eros and the Poet Philosopher." *Feminist Studies*, vol. 40, no. 1, 2014, pp. 169–189.

Gumbs, Alexis Pauline. "Repetition Is Sacred: School of Our Lorde, Mobile Homecoming, and Legacy in Flight." *Feminist Studies,* 40 no 1, 2014, pp. 207–215.

hooks, bell. "Theory as Liberatory Practice." *Yale Journal of Law and Feminism*, vol. 4, no. 1, 1991, pp.1-12.

Kelenyi, Gabrielle. "For the Love of Writing: Writing as a Form of (Self) Love." *Writers: Craft and Context,* vol. 2, no. 1, 2021, pp. 16-24.

Lindsay, Treva. "Beyond Surviving the Wholly Impossible: The Black Feminist Imperative of Joy." Visiting Black Intellectual Series, Butler University, 21 March 2023. Workshop.

Lorde, Audre. *Sister Outsider: Essays and Speeches.* Crossing Press, 1984.

Martinez, Aja Y. *Counterstory: The Rhetoric and Writing of Critical Race Theory.* CCCC/NCTE, 2020.

Milani, Tommaso M. "Fuck off! Recasting queer anger for a politics of (self-) discomfort." *Gender and Language,* vol. 15, no. 3, 2021, pp. 439-446.

Przybylo, Ela, and Kaiya Jacobs. "The Erotic Worldmaking of Asexual and Aromantic Zines." *QED: A Journal in GLBTQ Worldmaking,* vol. 8, no. 1, 2021, pp. 25-48.

Ore, Ersula, et al. "Diversity is not justice: working toward radical transformation and racial equity in the discipline." *College Composition and Communication*, vol. 72, no. 4, 2021, pp. 601-620.

—."Symposium: Diversity is not Enough: Mentorship and Community-Building as Antiracist Praxis", *Rhetoric Review*, vol. 40, no. 3, 2021, pp. 207-256.

Redden, Elizabeth. "Global Attack on Gender Studies." *Inside Higher Ed* , 4 Dec. 2018, www.insidehighered.com/news/2018/12/05/gender-studies-scholars-say-field-coming-under-attack-many-countries-around-globe.

Settles, Issa H, et al. "Epistemic Exclusion of Women Faculty and Faculty of Color: Understanding Scholar(ly) Devaluation as a Predictor of Turnover Intentions." *The Journal of Higher Education*, vol 93, no. 1, 2022, pp. 31-55.

Smythe, SA. "Can I Get a Witness? Black Feminism, Trans. Embodiment, and Thriving Past the Fault Lines of Care." *Palimpsest,* vol. 11, no. 1, 2022, pp. 85-107.

Toliver, S. R. "Can I Get a Witness? Speculative Fiction as Testimony and Counterstory." *Journal of Literacy Research,* vol. 52, no. 4, 2020, pp. 507–529.

Author Bio

Teigha VanHester (she/they) is an Assistant Professor of Race, Gender, and Sexuality Studies at Butler University in Indianapolis, IN. VanHester is currently an Emerging Scholar with Coalition for Community Writing and an Indiana Humanities Fellow. Their work has been published in *Race and Yoga*, *Women's Studies Quarterly*, and *Rhetorics, Politics, and Culture.* She completed her PhD in English Studies and a Women, Gender, Sexuality Studies Graduate Certificate at Illinois State University.

Issues in Community Literacy

Radically Imagining Community Programs: Reflection, Collaboration, and Organizer Toolkits

Erin Green

Abstract

This essay reflects on the challenges of facilitating a community program partnership with the Prince George's Memorial Library System. The program, "Community Justice," uses a public syllabus to introduce local teens to social justice concepts, theories, and methods. While issues of sustainability and retention are examined in this essay, much of the analysis centers on the community-engaged work of collaboration, reflection, and redesign. Additionally, this essay offers the field both an analysis of and a heuristic for teaching an under-explored community literacy utilized by activists: organizer toolkits.

Keywords: organizer toolkits, public syllabus, public library, teen activism, reflection

In the fall of 2022, I applied for a grant in my English department known as the Awards in the Public Humanities: Research & Engagement. The grant was presented by my department's Center for Literary and Comparative Studies (CLCS), a center that "showcases the research and creative activities of the department as well as helps develop new knowledge in literary and comparative studies" (*Center for Literary and Comparative Studies | Department of English*). That fall, I joined a cohort of researchers—graduate students and contingent faculty—who were asked to facilitate a public humanities project, specifically, a project that was meant to combine research and teaching to an audience beyond the university. I proposed a project, "Community Justice: Writing and Organizing for the Public," (which is shortened to "Community Justice" throughout this analysis) where I intended to use a public-facing syllabus as a heuristic to introduce public audiences to theories and practices of social justice. I planned to scaffold the syllabus with academic and public scholarship, community-engaged writing projects, collaborative workshops, and guest speakers. I intended "Community Justice" to allow participants to develop an anti-racist/social justice praxis, which I argued was critical to intervening in social justice issues within their communities.

While I had big goals for this project, as it was very ambitious, not all of my goals were accomplished. In this paper, I provide a reflective analysis of my experience—the trials and tribulations, cuz there was many—leading a public humanities project that centers community literacy and social justice. This paper explains that while I did not meet my goals for this project, I was able to adapt and reshape them to still enact radical change. I first review public humanities and community literacy scholarship and describe how it helped conceptualize my project. Briefly, I detail how I designed and redesigned my public humanities project and then reflect on how I responded and moved beyond those obstacles. I explain how I use a public syllabus—a freely accessible document that provides a reading list, political education, and resources to the public—as a starting point for constructing my community program. I end by providing resources that could be generative for community literacy practitioners.

Community literacy work is challenging and often comes with unforeseen disruptions. There is often an unbalance between university research and actual community engagement; therefore, finding that balance makes community literacy work arduous. My public humanities project tested me in ways academia had not, but it also provided me with a wealth of knowledge and experiences—even with my program being short-term—that encourages me to continue this kind of engagement. And too, this reflection offers me a chance to refigure my strategies before my next project and offers the field of community literacy an intervention for deepening our studies in a specific community literacy practice dedicated toward enacting radical change in our communities—organizer toolkits. More explicitly explained later in this paper, organizer toolkits are writing projects composed by community organizers and activists for community members to read and use as strategies for enacting change in their communities. "Community Justice" started as a public syllabus with the intention to engage the public about social justice issues. The public syllabus ultimately includes instruction and intellectual framing on why and how to create organizer toolkits. By focusing on these underexplored literacies, we have more ways in our work as community literacy practitioners to communicate, educate, and demand radical change.

Theories of Public Humanities and Community Literacy

Many public humanities and community literacy scholars have written extensively about the community-engaged work between writing teachers, community writing courses, and community members. In *African American Literacies*, Elaine Richardson argues that "the culturally biased education that most African Americans experience trains them to sever ties with Black communities and cultural activities. It trains us to have no interest in making a commitment to the uplift of other African Americans less fortunate than ourselves" (9). Many of our traditional academic writing courses are not geared towards engaging the communities of our students. Richardson's critique was a starting place for my community program. Additionally, I found Maisha Fisher's work in Black community literacies to be particularly helpful. She sought to

> understand how institution-building encouraged poets and writers to become educators, activists, community organizers, and leaders. Ideas, practices and values associated with literacy in these independent institutions often go unrecognized and undervalued in schools and formal institutions of teaching and learning… [These communities'] early literacy practices were

> not solely carried out for the purpose of leisure and enjoyment but they were political acts that could be considered early forms of institution-building (3, 14).

I wanted to frame my project as a collaborative process where I was working with community members to solve problems in their communities. My desire for this kind of program parallels that of Valerie Kinloch, Tanja Burkhard, and Carlotta Penn's "When School Is Not Enough: Understanding the Lives and Literacies of Black Youth." Specifically, they were interested in how Black youth used literacy to "interrogate their racialized experiences inside and outside school" and how they could "produce counternarratives to popular assumptions about Black youth from low-income urban communities" (Kinloch et al. 36). Knowing that the population of the teens attending the library branch where I facilitated my program were predominantly of color, I was invested in learning about their experiences as students of color in their schools and in their communities. Acting as co-investigators, I hoped to provide them with a space for reconciling with others about sociopolitical conditions that impacted their lives and with guidance for communicating their lived experiences, ideas, and political demands via writing. While my expertise in writing instruction, social movements, and antiracist activism certainly informed my conceptualization of the community program, my purpose was to provide space for discussion and reflection while also guiding them through a myriad of possible approaches of responding to those problems via writing.

My program focused on activists and social movements, and Black Lives Matter was just one of many social movements I planned for us to discuss during the program. Elaine Richardson and Alice Ragland have written about the power of the literacy practices of a movement like Black Lives Matter. They note that "BLM expands upon Black language traditions and creates its own semiotic system and literacy practices to signify pride, resilience, and affirmation of all Black humanity" (29). I wanted to combine both elements from "When School Is Not Enough" and Richardson and Ragland's piece where I provided the space for students to compose their experiences outside of a classroom and in the literacy practices of movements such as Black Lives Matter. As they argue, "Black literacies are based in the lived experiences of Black people" (31). Because of the historical context of racism happening in schools, whether it be linguistic racism towards different languages and literacies, or the banning of curriculum that centers people of color, students are often not given the space and opportunity to compose ideas and demands important to their lived experiences. My intentions were to create and facilitate that space for students in partnership with a community institution.

Despite this community literacy and public humanities scholarship being guiding principles for running my program, one of the major setbacks was learning to restructure it. The timeline of prepping this project consisted of approximately three months of me creating a syllabus, interacting with library workers, reflecting, redesigning my program, and collaborating with library workers on a separate, but similar, program. I expected to see 10-14 teens for an 8-week program. Between these 8 weeks, I had little to no attendance (2-3 participants). Participants did not attend for several reasons: some of them had sports practice, other extracurricular activities, or tutoring. Some of them may have decided to attend a different library event, some of them may have not had the transportation to be able to attend, or some of them may not have wanted to attend a program at all that day after spending eight hours in school. In addition to the challenge of attendance, planning engaging activities for only one to two people proved to also be difficult. While attendance prompted this reflection, the issue that I, a community literacy practitioner, had to solve was restructuring a program.

Designing the "Community Justice" Program

Before the program started, I initially thought my first step for designing this community program was to create the public facing syllabus, but in hindsight, I wish I had spent more time deciding on the intended audience, as this dilemma became the recurring issue for sustaining the program that I had originally proposed to the Center for Literary and Comparative Studies. I originally wanted to propose a community program to the Magic City Acceptance Academy, an LGBTQ-inclusive charter school in Alabama. My program would be geared towards students, faculty, and staff who wanted to enact radical change in their local communities as queer people and allies. In horror of what's currently happening in America with anti-transgender legislation, drag queen bans, and general queer hate crimes, I wish I would have been able to provide a queer-accepting school some resources to enact radical change in the South. As I write this, my home state of Alabama passed a law that "bans puberty blockers, hormone therapy and gender-affirming surgeries for minors" (Tryens-Fernandes). With this ongoing anti-queer oppression, a community program for queer Alabamians would have been helpful. In *Queer Literacies: Discourses and Discontents*, Mark McBeth theorizes that

> Throughout the twentieth century, the heteronormative literacy sponsorships (Pritchard's literacy normativities) gave rise to Queer advocacy groups and the rhetorical platforms they developed would dismantle the dominant heteronormative public voices (and the discourses that they espoused) that had prevailed over decades" (14).

Likewise in Alabama, the heteronormative literacy sponsors and discourses provided an exigence for me wanting to create a program to help queer people organize in the South. But because of the nature of public humanities work which includes administrative labor and bureaucratic necessities, I was not able to partner with the Magic City Acceptance Academy. As a Black queer Southerner, not being able to partner with the Academy and collaborate with them about queer activism is particularly disappointing as the United States continues with its onslaught of anti-trans legislation. In addition to bureaucratic necessities and administrative labor, I reflect on Travis Webster's book, *Queerly Centered: LGBTQA Writing Center Directors Navigate the Workplace*, in which he describes the queer labor and (in)visible work queer writing center directors must perform, especially in moments of violence against queer people. Specifically, he thinks about "the ways queer writing center labor intersects with national issues that impact people of difference" (5). Noting the *Pulse* nightclub shooting as just one example, violence against queer people prompted Webster "to inquire deeply, personally, into queer leadership in the writing center field, alongside but also far beyond the work of peer writing tutoring" (5). Additionally, Webster's analysis of the community-oriented work that LGBTQ+ writing center directors feel compelled to do parallels my motivation for facilitating "Community Justice."

With the current political discourse delegitimizing critical race theory, Black History, and social justice initiatives, "Community Justice" was meant to be more than just a program for students to write outside of school. Conceptualizing writing center work as more than just peer tutoring is also described in Laura Greenfield's *Radical Writing Center Praxis*, in which she argues for writing center workers to engage their communities to enact change. With my positionality as a Black queer Southerner, I knew the labor of helping other queer Southerners would have been challenging, but worthwhile. Because I was under a time constraint though, I had to find another community quickly to partner with to facilitate my program: Prince George's County Memorial Library System (PGCMLS).

Public Syllabi

Much of my doctoral research involves community-engaged and activist writing, Black queer literacies, critical race theory, storytelling, and abolition. Because of these research interests, I have read several public syllabi or artifacts that I would classify as public syllabi. These include Candice Benbow's *Lemonade Syllabus*, a collection of readings and resources centering Black womanhood; the African American Intellectual Historical Society's prison abolition syllabi; and the Social Science Research Council's *#coronavirussyllabus*. Additionally, as a scholar studying social movements and abolition, I have reviewed several community organizer toolkits that operate as public syllabi. The goal of a public syllabus should be for anyone to be able to physically access it and for the syllabus readings to also be accessible. This usually means most of the reading should not exist behind a paywall or only be accessible via a university account. Additionally, the public syllabus should be flexible for anyone to be able to pick up, read, and comprehend. There should be no perquisites for the public syllabus as the audience in mind is a general public audience with an interest in the subject matter. While there can be "suggested reading" as a way for viewers to be able to contextualize some of the material, it should not be totally necessary. Because of my background as a college instructor though, my public syllabus read as a syllabus for the standard college course, not for a community program beyond the academy. Normally where a course description would be located, I added a "program description" that read as follows:

> Since 2020, many people have become energized by social justice initiatives to become activists and engage in community organizing. From police abolition, and reproductive justice, to climate action, and more—communities have always been at the forefront of movements seeking to enact social

change. While social media activism is a highly successful tool in spreading awareness, it is but one form of activism.

This 8-week community program—one hour weekly—invites Prince George's County community members to learn theoretical arguments about concepts like capitalism/neoliberalism or the prison-industrial complex and learn practical strategies for community engagement: grassroots organizing, coalition building, and restorative/transformative justice. In this program, we will explore the difference between an activist and a community organizer. Using an "asset-based" community development model, this program provides members a space for them to intervene—as experts—in an issue within their own communities, develop a praxis informed by scholarship of antiracism and enact social change through community-engaged writing and radical imagination.

To mirror the standard college course syllabus even more, I added what would normally be considered "learning outcomes," but phrased it as "program outcomes." Specifically, I said:

Members of the program can expect to:

- Learn the histories of different activists and social movements
- Understand different theories and arguments of antiracism and social justice
- Identify sociopolitical issues in their communities
- Engage with different activist strategies and organizer toolkits
- Develop strategies to build a coalition for their issues
- Collaborate with other community members
- Create community-engaged writing projects
- Participate in collaborative writing workshops
- Attend guest speaker lectures
- Develop an activist/organizer identity
- Intervene, via writing, in their communities to address sociopolitical issues

Framing this project as a community program that was supposed to exist outside of the university, but still using the language, frameworks, and designs that I would normally use in a college course clearly misses the point of this program existing outside the university. Even though the content of the program centers social justice activism in communities, I was still relying on the practices and tools needed to structure a college course, not a community program. I created a "program calendar" that detailed the theme for every week, the assigned reading, and a deliverable. Once I was able to establish a partnership with the PGCMLS, I realized that I needed to drastically rethink and restructure the community program that I facilitated.

PGCMLS has a program called Teen Action Group (TAG) that is "a monthly meeting that focuses on community-based programs and service-learning opportunities" (*Teen Action Group (TAG) - Prince George's County Memorial Library System*). As I was designing the program before it started, I made plans to visit one of their meetings to advertise the community justice writing program. In addition to strategizing registration, I inquired with the PGCMLS area manager on how to run a community program for teens, as it would be different than running a college classroom. She recommended I focus on providing an experiential learning experience. This included icebreakers, hands-on activities, and interactive learning. As a composition teacher and writing program administrator, I had always seen the value in a scaffolded curriculum, and the community program I had designed relied on scaffolded reading and writing projects. Because community literacy practitioners must be adaptable, I chose to redesign the structure of my program to accommodate my participants' various lives. Instead of scaffolding the community program, I redesigned the program to be a different topic and different writing activity each week. I decided to "lesson plan" one week in advance so that I could account for what was successful and unsuccessful. By deciding not to scaffold the community program, I was able to ensure that each week participants could learn something and contribute without having to have been at previous meetings. Another element I had to employ when transforming the program's academic-oriented syllabus to a public-facing syllabus was the exclusion of assigned readings. Because I wanted to emulate the flexibility of public syllabi where anyone could teach it and anyone could show up, having an assigned reading before the program would be more of a hindrance. Additionally, I didn't want to replicate the same educational environment that they had just left at their high schools.

Reciprocity and Redesign

My redesign process occurred after I had already created the public syllabus and was running "Community Justice." As I was working on redesigning my program from its original syllabus, I was able to get in contact with an additional library worker who specialized in Teen Services. This library specialist had previously coordinated a Social Justice Summer Camp and asked if I would like to get involved. I met with him and a cohort of other library workers to prepare for the summer camp. While I was still running my own community program in the spring, I was simultaneously writing the curriculum for the library's eventual summer camp. It was during these meetings that I was able to see that there was one key element that was missing from my community program: collaboration. PGCMLS's Social Justice Summer Camp "helps teens ages 13 to 17 learn not only about advocacy but also how to conduct research and learn the fundamentals of public speaking and other skills to improve the quality of their communities" (Ford). The camp's coordinator enlisted library workers, and me, to create a camp curriculum of modules pertaining to the camp's mission. Modules for the camp include Research, Ethics, Problem Solving, History of Social Justice, and Social Entrepreneurship & Enterprise. I chose to create the Activists and Advocates module because it was a similar topic to the community program that I was already facilitating through my CLCS grant. For my module, I needed to compose an overview of the unit, provide one hour worth of activities, materials for the facilitator, and resources. I helped with designing their Social Justice Summer Camp. After "Community Justice" ended in March, I continued helping design PGCMLS's Social Justice Summer Camp and even led two sessions in the summer. Helping with this camp was beneficial for me because I was able to take what I learned from these library workers who had already facilitated a community program in a non-college setting. They were the experts in this situation, and I greatly relied on their expertise.

This collaboration with community members and experts outside of academia allowed me to experience another concept prominent in community literacy scholarship: reciprocity. As Jennifer Bay argues in her article on research justice: "academics, as experienced researchers, have a unique perspective and skill: research. Research is an essential part of many writing projects, and as scholars, we have a commitment to our own research, which sometimes conflicts with community projects or partnerships" (10). Even as I collaborated with the library workers and their community program and recognized their expertise and supported how they defined our relationship, this process did not always align with my own research and what I hoped to gain from working with them. Because of the capitalistic nature of academia necessitating a publication as a way to represent my labor and value, community literacy researchers can be placed in a difficult position in wanting the purpose of our work to primarily be serving the communities in which we're collaborating while also collecting data and experiences to support our research. Bay describes the nuances of reciprocity when doing community-engaged work. She states that "overcoming the power dynamics between the university and community may limit the ability for true reciprocity to occur" (11). The power dynamics for the Summer Camp were clearly defined: I was a volunteer helping the library facilitate their program. While establishing this relationship, the library workers also offered their assistance with any of my research. While it might be easy for community literacy researchers to see the outcome of a partnership to be reciprocity, Bay offers an approach that turns "away from the idea of reciprocity as an ultimate goal and toward the idea of research justice to show how sometimes we must rethink our methods and our outcomes to respond in humane ways to those we work with in the community" (11). Reflecting on my time with the PGCMLS, I think about how our goal of working together was not reciprocity, but ultimately was to provide a community program for teens to learn about social justice. Reciprocity was just one method for creating the program. By exchanging our levels of expertise, we were able to create a summer camp, gain an extra set of hands in conceptualizing the modules and logistics of the camp, and have a conversation for a research symposium at my university about the camp. I had hoped to co-author this article with PGCMLS about our work together, but bureaucratic red tape prevented us from doing so. As community literacy researchers continue to do community-engaged work, we should adopt Bay's approach of research justice, specifically turning away from reciprocity as the end goal and toward reciprocity as a method to enact radical change.

Laurie JC Cella and Jessica Restaino's introduction to their book, *Unsustainable: Re-imagining Community Literacy, Public Writing, Service-Learning, and the University*, provides generative thoughts on how I saw my community program being sustained after the completion of my public humanities project. One suggestion Cella and Restaino offer is to see that "both long- and short-term projects have value," therefore, we "need to deepen our understanding of successful projects, and include the semester-long project in the spectrum of successful community literacy projects" (2). While my project ran from January to May of 2023, I too want to acknowledge the flexibility of sustainability in short-term programs when we approach sustainability based on the needs of the community. I may not be able to continue to run my former community program with the same resources, but there are ways for me to continue to sustain the ideals and principles of my program with that community: volunteering to create modules for the Social Justice Camp, helping recruit teens, highlighting PGCMLS's social justice work, and creating resources for them to use in their own programming.

Organizer Toolkits

If my program had better attendance, I would have ended it with a collaboratively curated community organizer and activist toolkit. Many community organizers have published digital toolkits for engaging and organizing their communities around specific social movements. Organizer toolkits are promising sites for community literacy analysis as they are written by community members for community members prompting action for social and radical change. For example, Critical Resistance is an organization working towards community-based approaches to dismantling the prison-industrial complex, specifically addressing issues of police brutality, mass incarceration, and interpersonal violence. One of their organizer toolkits is *Our Communities, Our Solutions: An Organizer's Toolkit for Developing Campaigns to Abolish Policing* and

> In this toolkit, you will find **tools for talking about policing from a [prison-industrial complex] abolitionist perspective**—including ***definitions of policing*** and ***abolition***, along with key terms often referred to or needed in this moment, and **sample talking points** on defunding police. You will also find tools aimed at helping more communities **strengthen our organizing to meet this moment** and carry our movement beyond, specifically in the demands [they] work to win or challenge and the **campaign planning and development** we need to do in order to move more deliberately and collectively toward liberation. [They] have also included recommended **political education materials and resources** for further study, as well as **examples of past statements on policing**, a tactic [their] chapters have used throughout the years in building resistance to policing (emphasis in original, Critical Resistance 4).

Not only are these toolkits showcasing the kind of community literacies and community-engaged writing associated with radical change work, but they are also underexplored artifacts that can advance both community literacy scholarship and community literacy work. Fisher states that "Literacy and knowledge were the key tenets of revolutionary action. One had to be well-read in literature, and history but most importantly one had to be willing to organize and take action" (86). My inclusion of organizer toolkits parallels her argument. While these toolkits are underexplored sites for community literacy scholars, the toolkits' most important purpose is to be a resource to enact radical change in communities. Therefore, to study these toolkits without any intention of using them to dismantle the very oppressive systems affecting our communities would be deliberately dismissing the intended purpose of these community documents. I argue for using these toolkits as they were intended and not just as "writing assignments" because these toolkits can truly transform our students' communities and even our communities. These toolkits are resources for resisting police violence, incarceration, poverty, interpersonal violence, criminalization, and more. Because these toolkits, for many, address sociopolitical issues of life or death, we should not take them for granted as just writing assignments for our community-engaged classrooms, but as tools that have the potential to enact radical change.

Teachers of community-engaged and public writing courses can mirror the very literacy practices employed by community organizers, activists, and educators working toward change in their communities. Many of the organizations publishing toolkits are radical agents of change, supporting political visions of abolition, anti-capitalism, antiracism, anti-imperialism, socialism, communism, anarchism, and feminism. Organizations like Advancement Project, Community Justice Exchange, Creative Interventions, Critical Resistance, Dream Defenders, Interrupting Criminalization, MPD150, Transform Harm, Vision Change Win, and Beyond Criminal Courts are community-oriented organizations and movements publishing these toolkits for community members to use in their own communities. A particular toolkit that community-engaged writing instructors might find useful for their students to read and use in their campus communities is Advancement Project's *We Came to Learn: A Call to Action for Police-Free Schools*. Instructors can use this toolkit as reading materials for their courses before asking them to create their own.

This toolkit seeks to "Offer a deep dive and analysis of the history and legacy of school policing" so students will gain the knowledge about school policing (Alliance for Educational Justice 2). The toolkit also seeks to "Equip communities with tools to access school police data and budgets, and understand the oversight and governance structures (if any) of school police infrastructure(s) in [their] districts and cities" (2). Students could very well take the reading outside of their class and use it alongside their peers to organize their communities to get cops off campus. Instructors should certainly be a part of this campaign since college campuses are our communities as well.

The benefit of a public syllabus like "Community Justice," is that it was not intended to be exclusive to a classroom. Public syllabi are constructed for community members and since many are free to access, a public syllabus offers the public instructions on specific activist literacy practices. Many organizer toolkits contain instructions for how to transform our communities through numerous methods, but many do not have instructions on how to create the organizer toolkit itself. A genre like public syllabi provides the political education necessary for constructing an organizer toolkit. Creating and distributing organizer toolkits is just one strategy of enacting radical change. To highlight these underexplored literacies, I provide guidelines for how I would have facilitated this writing project in my community program. These guidelines can be adopted by community literacy practitioners wanting to run their own writing-centered program or by composition instructors teaching community-engaged writing courses. Teaching community members and students how to craft these documents, which are meant for radical change, is an invaluable way for our field to stress community literacies as emergent strategies.

While there is no right or wrong way to construct an organizer toolkit, or how to teach others how to construct one, the steps I provide in this section are a good starting point. To compose an organizer toolkit, writers should pick an issue currently affecting their community. For example, during my community program, I learned that substance abuse and gun violence were prominent issues in my teen's communities. Since most toolkits are co-authored, I recommend collaboration rather than individually authored toolkits. I also recommend collaboration because community organizing is inherently collaborative work. Concerning the contents of the toolkit, I recommend starting with a brief definition of organizing, identification and description of the community's issue, explanation of the solution(s) to the issue, strategies (i.e., campaign tools, political education resources, statements to legislatures, fundraising ideas, workshop materials, data collection, coalition building practices, public records requests, demonstrations and protests, risk assessment, restorative practices, transformative justice, etc.), and ways for people to get in contact with the composers or more involved in the movement. Because composing an organizer toolkit is so research and writing intensive, I do not recommend assigning this as a "final writing project" 2-3 weeks before the end of the semester. In fact, I would make the organizer toolkit the sole project for the course and break the toolkit into separate writing tasks throughout the semester. This scaffolded approach allows students to work on the organizer toolkit throughout the semester and can be divided into five separate writing projects: definition of organizing; community issue; community solution(s); organizing strategies; and dissemination.

The Urban Institute defines community organizing as "a method for building power, particularly for people and communities who have traditionally been excluded from decisionmaking […] it involves community organizers working to build grassroots leadership to create and advocate for policy solutions and changes to systems that produce inequities" (Urban Institute). Students could conduct traditional academic research to familiarize themselves with community organizing as a concept and practice, or instructors could assign readings and lecture on them, but a more practical way would be inviting community organizers themselves to come speak about their work. Inviting organizers to speak about their work, both legitimizes their roles as experts and allows students, or community members, to acquire real engagement with people in their community already in the process of enacting radical change. Students should choose academic, social, or political issues that are important to their communities and that they are interested in solving. Examples of issues affecting college students could be Advancement Project's toolkit on getting cops out of schools—or in our case off campus. Students creating a cop-free campus toolkit might decide that one solution is defunding campus police and reallocating those funds to student-centered services. This solution could be completed through a multitude of organizing strategies. Part of the toolkit could include students doing data collection on campus police to determine how much the police are funded, the training necessary for the police, and even instances of police violence on campus. Another strategy could be students offering materials to compose statements to the university administration and even the city legislature. Students could offer strategies for student groups or organizations wanting to do effective campus demonstrations. Think of this as "the dos and don'ts of protesting on campus." Last, students could offer strategies on how students could gravitate toward restorative and transformative justice approaches to deal with harm instead of involving campus police. Students still learn the fundamentals of rhetoric-based writing by paying close attention to audience, purpose, exigence, and style; however, with the organizer toolkits, they have a chance to engage in the same community literacy practices as community organizers and activists with the hopes of securing some form of social or political change in their communities. The same goes for members of a community program that centers writing and organizing. When "Community Justice" did have attendance, a common issue my teen participants brought up was gun violence. I could very well imagine the participants collaboratively constructing an organizer toolkit about how to address gun violence in Prince George's County high schools. We would have gone through the same steps I described above with the intention for this document to be put to real use and for it to be distributed to their communities.

Most organizer toolkits are distributed digitally by organizations. Since my students did not have their own organizations, I would have recommended they host their documents in a place with open access (e.g., Google Drive or a website). They could distribute it digitally through social media, neighborhood listservs, and other organizations that they're members of. They could also hold their own meetings in their schools or at public places like public libraries to discuss their toolkits. In a community-engaged writing course, students have numerous ways to disseminate their organizer toolkits. With the cop-free campus example, students could promote their toolkits with the campus newspaper(s), campus radio, student group meetings, student government association meetings and events. Students can also spread it via word of mouth and through printed copies of the toolkit. QR codes linking to the toolkit posted in various locations on campus are also effective. The instructor of the community-engaged writing course should also be involved in the toolkit's distribution. Various ways for the instructor to distribute include posting it on the departmental websites, sending it to faculty members, advocating for it at faculty senate or department/university-wide committees, and promoting it at events in our own communities. Again, the purpose of the toolkit—even in a college course—is not to simply write about these strategies and tools for organizing. The purpose is to use this writing to achieve direct action that helps dismantle some form of oppression and transform communities into more equitable places.

Conclusion

Even though I didn't get a chance to teach my participants how to compose organizer toolkits, I'm happy I had the chance to facilitate "Community Justice" because it provided me with the opportunity to work with other experts in community-engaged work outside of the academy. Partnering with PGCMLS was a life-changing experience for me as a community literacy researcher as it helped develop my role as a scholar-teacher-activist. I felt like I saw tangible results by doing social justice work in communities outside of the academy. Had it not been for my willingness to adapt and restructure, I would not have gotten to experience helping with the Social Justice Summer Camp. On the very last day of the Social Justice Summer Camp, I got to see all of the teens pitch social justice initiatives and ideas to a group of stakeholders. These stakeholders were members of the students' communities who worked in non-profits, non-governmental organizations, legal centers, and education. They were all genuinely interested in hearing what issues were impacting the teens' communities and what they thought should be done about it. After teens submitted their pitches to the stakeholders, they were provided feedback and resources for the next steps for continuing their social justice work. The summation of the work that these teens had done included identifying problems in their own communities, learning about advocacy organizations and organizers in their local communities, and learning about the various methods activists and organizers use to enact change. Seeing the work that these teens had done and how connected it was to their local communities was an enriching experience for me because a lot of social justice efforts—even in community writing classrooms—in academia can seem so distant from the communities in which they're engaging.

The more I reflect on "Community Justice" the more I realize that the Social Justice Summer Camp was exactly what I was striving to provide: a space for teens to be able to learn about important concepts and methods of social justice movements and to guide teens through a written projects where they are experts in their communities advocating for specific changes. I hope to try again one day with a community program because I know the organizer toolkits, and other literacies from organizers and activists, are sites and practices worth not only studying, but teaching others and utilizing so that radical change can be made in our communities. Additionally, I look forward to using this public syllabus during my own community-engaged college writing courses, and most definitely using the cops-off-campus toolkit to introduce the genre. As the field of community literacy progresses, we must continue to not only study the language and literacy practices of activists and organizers, but also adopt these practices to transform our communities. And as community program facilitators, we must continue to rethink what our goals are for community programs. Establishing goals beyond reciprocity can move community literacy practitioners toward more emergent strategies for enacting radical change. Last, as we continue to amplify the language and literacy practices of activists and organizers—like public syllabi and organizer toolkits—we, community literacy researchers-teachers, must not leave the activism and community organizing solely to non-academic community members. For many of us, these are our communities as well, so we should see ourselves as a part of social movements bringing forth social justice initiatives in collaboration with the public. We owe our time and labor to the communities we study, write about, engage with, and even call home by working alongside the activists and organizers who have been committed to enacting radical change.

Works Cited

Alliance for Educational Justice. *We Came to Learn: A Call to Action for Police-Free Schools*. Advancement Project, 2023.

Bay, Jennifer. "Research Justice as Reciprocity: Homegrown Research Methodologies Methodologies." *Community Literacy Journal*, vol. 14, no. 1, 2019, pp. 7–25.

Cella, Laurie JC. "Introduction: Taking Stock of Our Past and Assessing the Future of Community Writing Work." *Unsustainable: Re-Imagining Community Literacy, Public Writing, Service-Learning, and the University*, edited by Laurie JC Cella and Jessica Restaino, Lexington Books, 2012, pp. 1–14.

Center for Literary and Comparative Studies | Department of English. 15 Mar. 2023, english.umd.edu/research-innovation/clcs.

Critical Resistance. *Our Communities, Our Solutions: An Organizer's Toolkit for Developing Campaigns to Abolish Policing*. Critical Resistance, 2020, criticalresistance.org/resources/our-communities-our-solutions-an-organizers-toolkit-for-developing-campaigns-to-abolish-policing/.

Fisher, Maisha. *Black Literate Lives: Historical and Contemporary Perspectives*. Routledge, 2009.

Ford, William J. "Teens Learn Advocacy, Research at Social Justice Camp in Prince George's." *The Washington Informer*, 3 Aug. 2022, www.washingtoninformer.com/teens-learn-advocacy-research-at-social-justice-camp-in-prince-georges/.

Kinloch, Valerie, et al. "When School Is Not Enough: Understand the Lives and Literacies of Black Youth." *Research in the Teaching of English*, vol. 52, no. 1, 2017, pp. 34–54.

McBeth, Mark. *Queer Literacies: Discourses and Discontents*. Lexington Books, 2019.

Richardson, Elaine. *African American Literacies*. Routledge, 2002.

Richardson, Elaine, and Alice Ragland. "#StayWoke: The Language and Literacies of the #BlackLivesMatter Movement." *Community Literacy Journal*, vol. 12, no. 2, 2018, pp. 27–56.

Teen Action Group (TAG) - Prince George's County Memorial Library System. www.pgcmls.info/tag. Accessed 28 Mar. 2023.

Tryens-Fernandes, Savannah. "Judge Requires Parents to Turn over Transgender Children's Medical Records." *AL.Com*, 27 Mar. 2023, www.al.com/educationlab/2023/03/judge-requires-parents-to-turn-over-transgender-childrens-medical-records.html.

Urban Institute. "Community Organizing." *Pursuing Housing Justice: Interventions for Impact*, 2023, www.urban.org/apps/pursuing-housing-justice-interventions-impact/community-organizing.

Webster, Travis. *Queerly Centered: LGBTQA Writing Center Directors Navigate the Workplace*. Utah State UP, 2021.

Author Bio

Erin Green is a PhD Candidate at the University of Maryland studying Language, Writing, and Rhetoric. Their research interests include literacy studies, composition theory, writing program administration, and community-engaged writing. Their current dissertation research examines the various community literacy practices of abolitionist activists and organizers.

Book and New Media Reviews

From the Book and New Media Review Editor's Desk

Jessica Shumake, Editor
University of Notre Dame

It is possible to experience kindness, creativity, and joy when one least expects it. The day before the Conference on Community Writing (CCW) in Denver in October, I walked to Leven Deli before exploring the Denver Art Museum (DAM) with my two-year-old and four-month-old. The line at Leven Deli snaked out the door, yet before my two-year-old's impatient tugs at my leg became a meltdown, an employee approached us, complimenting the goldfish print on my shirt, surprisingly visible underneath the infant I carried in a front pack. Despite our position toward the back of the line, we were asked what we would like to eat from the menu, which I craned my neck to read. My hyperverbal two-year-old chimed in with, "How about a treat?" The Leven employee smiled and asked, "Would you like to try a tahini brownie?" My two-year-old agreed and I nodded enthusiastically. Instead of a sample, we were handed an enormous brownie in a paper to-go bag. Astonished, I asked, "How much do I owe you?" The response left me speechless, "Nothing. I want you to enjoy it. I hope you have fun today." This gesture of kindness delighted my hungry toddler and caused tears to well in my eyes, which I hoped no one noticed. The drive to Denver from South Bend, with an infant and a toddler, depleted me and it felt miraculous that the three of us made it out of our hotel room before noon amid nursing, bathing, diapering, and dressing. The Leven employee saw me and my children in all our wobbliness and met us with joy and generosity. I felt myself buoyed to face any obstacles I met that day and called to write about how the gift of recognition and a delicious treat contributed to my felt sense that I could be out in the world with two small humans doing something fun—amid diaper blowouts and soaked nursing pads—while my spouse worked in the business center at the hotel. Savoring the brownie and its crunchy tahini morsels, my son, inspired by video clips of Amoako Boafo finger painting, created a messy but heartfelt collage at the Creative Hub in the DAM, which is a space for hands-on artmaking. Upon our later return to the deli with the gift of the collage in hand, the Leven employee asked my two-year-old to sign it, saying, "When you're a famous artist, I want to be able to tell people I have one of your early works." My two-year-old beamed and drew a line with a pen that barely resembled a signature. The hunt for Leven's perfect brownie continues, fueled by a new metal pan and the memory of unexpected kindness.

The reviewers featured in this issue, Michael Harker and Jamie D. I. Duncan, both offer insightful nourishment for *CLJ* readers. I hope you appreciate their reviews and that their writing inspires broad engagement with scholarship in community writing.

Unsettling Archival Research: Engaging Critical, Communal, and Digital Archives

Edited by Gesa E. Kirsch, Romeo García, Caitlin Burns Allen, and Walker P. Smith. Southern Illinois University Press, 2023, 321 pp.

Reviewed by Michael Harker
Georgia State University

In her foundational work "Autobiography of an Archivist," Nan Johnson writes: "I stared and stared around the rim of signs, around the wheel of stacks. With astonishment, I realized there was no center to my wheel. All the stacks seemed to be pointing inward to something. What was it?" (295). Johnson's description of this moment captures the vexing and dynamic nature of archival research. It also reveals her infectious enthusiasm and deep affinity for archival labor, an energy that would inspire and sustain a generation of scholars participating in the archival turn in rhetoric and writing studies. Johnson's quest to find the center of her unpacked stacks of primary sources will not only culminate in her meticulously documented *Gender and Rhetorical Space in American Life: 1866–1910,* but it will also pave the way for the development of her research heuristic: The Archival Wheel. In both form and function, Johnson's Archival Wheel marks a pedagogical and methodological moment with respect to our field's engagement with archives, one we might understand in terms of a need to identify singular and all-encompassing narratives within archives.

In their new collection, *Unsettling Archival Research: Engaging Critical, Communal, and Digital Archives,* Gesa E. Kirsch, Romeo García, Caitlin Burns Allen, and Walker P. Smith offer a powerful and unsettling dimension to Johnson's heuristic. Rather than pursuing a definitive, unifying, or centered response to the question "What is it?" as the starting point for meaning-making in archival research and historiography, the editor's introduction emphasizes instability and purposeful disruption of centering as a foundational principle for contemporary archival studies. "Once more," the editors note: "*Unsettling Archival Research* means peeling back the layers of what is constituted as settled so as to be able to witness, (re)orient oneself to, and carefully reckon with wounded/ing and haunted/ing spaces, places, and memories" (4). Linked directly with "the current political, environmental, social, and historical moment" this collection offers welcomed immediacy and bold questions aimed toward destabilizing established archival research conventions. It also reveals a unifying spirit of advocacy and bearing witness in service of the purpose of the collection—to demonstrate how archives serve "as a powerful medium for bearing witness in unsettling ways" (9).

Key to sustaining this collection's thesis is bringing to bear on prevailing approaches to archival research and historiography the guiding questions, theories, tensions, and methodologies of critical archival studies. The editors and contributors appropriately position Michelle Caswell as a leading voice in contemporary archival research and historiography. Caswell's persistent calls to acknowledge the intellectual contributions of archival studies appear throughout the collection, serving as a reference point for a collection determined to unsettle archival research. Doing so makes possible additional goals for the collection, including "to present a new vision of archival research—one that invites understanding of small-a archives beyond institutional Archives" (8). As a result, the collection foregrounds engagement with archives broadly defined and encompasses "a wide variety of venues, including institutional and community archives, archival ephemera, case studies, oral histories, and interviews. . ." (11). With such diverse evidentiary practices and an explicit focus on unsettling key concepts, theories, and perspectives, it would be easy for readers to struggle to navigate the text. However, the introduction to the collection provides readers with a clear explanation of the collection's guiding questions and, perhaps most importantly, acknowledgment of the many rhetoric and writing studies scholars who have provided the language and orientation to engage with archival studies in the first place.

The core focus of part one, "Unsettling Key Concepts," is to question underlying assumptions that have traditionally guided archival work. The starting point for the collection is remarkable for how effectively it disrupts entrenched and conventional receptions of key terms in archival studies. Here, mainstays of archival studies like "story," "provenance," and "rescue," which have traditionally steered the field, are interrogated and jostled off-center, unsettling the alignment of conventions that have informed rhetoric and writing studies' engagement with archival studies. In chapter one, "Unsettling the 'Archive Story,'" Jean Bessette sets the tone for the entire collection by reframing a question implicitly accepted in archival studies: "What's in a story?" Bessette's inquiry upends entrenched tropes of archival studies to carve out a space for alternative characterizations. In this instance, her framing of narrative serves as a reminder that "stories within the archive are less directly centered on the archive itself and more reflective of the researcher's individual experience" (30). Teacher-researchers seeking a rhetorical understanding of narrative in the context of archival research will find this chapter valuable for its direct engagement with the work of James Phelan and Peter J. Rabinowitz. In chapter two, "Rescuing the Archive from What?" Wendy Hayden interrogates the theoretical, thematic, social, and disciplinary underpinnings of "rescuing" as a methodology for archival research. Although Hayden acknowledges the importance of the metaphor of rescuing as an organizing statement for the field as it initially engaged with archives, she notes that researchers have moved past such conceptions, offering Ann Cvetovich's research as well as Jessica Enoch and Jordynn Jack's scholarship as examples. She questions the tendency of researchers who unintentionally characterize their role as heroic in the research process. The idea of rescuing, Hayden argues, has greater value as a pedagogical orientation for students who benefit from lessons learned critiquing the approach more generally (40).

In chapter three, "Narratives of Triumph: A Case Studies of the Polio Archive," Jackie M. James offers a "project of reparative justice" with the purpose of unsettling "erased histories" (49). Employing "kairology as a methodological approach," James amplifies the stories and materiality of polio narratives that have been overlooked and excluded. She utilizes kairology, focusing on "fitness-to-situation" (50), to explore more nuanced questions beyond merely identifying absent elements within archives. James contends that critical archival researchers must come to terms with the reasons behind the absence of specific aspects of records. A central question of her proposed approach is: "Why are the materials in the archive? What do the physical contents of the collection say about what was valued in this history and what was not?" (50). In chapter four, Kalyn Prince's methodological approach, "critical nostalgia," aims to assist researchers in reconciling ideological tensions that often lead to discomfort in bearing witness to historical records. In "Nostalgia in the Archives: Using Nostalgia as a Tool for Negotiating Ideological Tensions," Prince offers readers a brief but useful interrogation of the term "nostalgia," tracing it back to its Greek roots. Among the most important chapters in the collection, Prince offers readers a more complete understanding of nostalgia that underscores its rhetorical potential, centrality, and complexity as a tool for achieving the shared goal of unsettling archival research (64).

In chapter five, "A Matter of Order: The Power of Provenance in the Mercury Collection of Marion Lamm," Kathryn Manis and Patty Wilde extend established critiques of provenance, "a shibboleth of archival studies," prioritizing how "provenance operates as an episteme coloniality" (67). Amplifying the work of Cushman and García, the authors do not mince words when it comes to what they describe as problems with provenance (68). "Born from a system," the authors write, "that privileges white, weatherly, cisgendered, heterosexual males, provenance prioritizes knowledge produced by the powerful. . ." (70). Teacher-researchers seeking an instructive discussion of how provenance can center some voices and viewpoints while subjugating others" (70) will find Manis and Wilde's discussion of the Mercury Collection of Marion Lamm valuable.

Part two, "Unsettling Research, Theory, and Methodology," addresses tensions frequently encountered in the archival research process. Although the contributors' scopes, methodologies, and evidence differ considerably in this section, a unifying element is the profound influence and adherence to Michelle Caswell's recommendations. In chapter six, "Hidden in Plain Sight: Rescuing the Archives from Disciplinarity," Lynée Lewis Gaillet and Jessica A. Rose present two case studies of community activism, the AIDS Quilt and the community activism of Dorothy Bolden, organizer of the National Domestic Workers Union. More than other contributions in this section, this chapter actively embraces and embodies Caswell's call for increased collaboration between humanities scholars and information specialists (85). For instance, Gaillet and Rose draw threads from the Society of American Archivists (SAA) Core Values and Code of Ethics, situating it as a point of reference for preparing the next generation of archival researchers, "especially those," they write, "investigating social justice issues" (84). Teacher-researchers seeking out language and evidence to support establishing pedagogical connections to archival research will appreciate this chapter. Gaillet and Rose conclude that "instruction in archival methodologies, community activism, and archiving practices" is key to developing, establishing, and sustaining the types of coalitions and collaborations that exemplify the spirit of critical archival studies. In line with recommendations from the previous chapter, María Pas Carvajal Regidor's "(En)Countering Archival Silences: Critical Lenses, Relationships, and Informal Archives" argues for the importance of informal archives connected with critical race theory (CRT). For Regidor, informal archives are comprised of materials that "have been collected or left by multiple individuals and not organized or curated in a systematic way" (107). The literacy practices and values of Latinx/Latine students are at stake in bearing witness to trends and the larger socio-historical context of informal archives. Evidence of these values, Regidor argues, is often elided by the research and preservation practices associated with more formal archives (121).

The thematic focus of silence, absence, and the incompleteness of historical records take center stage in the latter portions of part two. The final three chapters in this section actively employ broadened and refigured characterizations of provenance, revealing Caswell's profound influence on the collection more generally. In chapter eight, "Let Them Speak: Rhetorically Reimagining Prison Voices in the Archives of the Collective," Sally F. Benson's engagement with the archives of the Penitentiary of New Mexico leads her to draw an important distinction between silence and absence. "Archival silences," she writes, "represent 'void regions' of unheard stories that haunt our history" (Carter qtd. in Benson 129). Benson's archival research and commitment to ethics demonstrate how incarcerated individuals have been historically neglected, highlighting further the need for critical archival perspectives on prison archives. Such an approach, she contends, serves to acknowledge the rhetorical agency of incarcerated residents/journalists and confront "public misunderstanding of who is in our prisons" (143). In chapter nine, "Bearing Witness to Transient Histories," Pamela Takayoshi embraces most fully the spirit of the collection, investigating the "fragmentary record of mental healthcare" of nineteenth-century women's experiences in American insane asylums. Significant for its lucid and strategic contemplation on "Reconstructing Intersectional Positionality," this chapter connects the priorities of critical archival studies to identity, a term often narrowly understood as representing individual experiences instead of "transpersonal and interpersonal sets of privileges and oppressions" (159). The result of this approach is an exemplary model of bearing witness to archival work that makes legible the invisible forces that beckon critical researchers to reconstruct the transient, incomplete, and uneven histories of marginalized people.

Walker P. Smith's impressive tenth chapter, "The Rhetorical (Im)possibilities of Recovering George Barr: Toward a Decolonial Queer Archival Methodology," throws into relief nuanced lessons of critical archival approaches conveyed in both part one and part two, but not simply for the sake of doing so. Smith's case study of George Barr's artwork upsets the expected outputs of queer historical interpretations by resisting "making legible and reproducible our settled, symmetrical hierarchy of new, newer, and newest versions of queer history" (180). In arguing for a pluriversal relationality aimed toward opposing the "modern/colonial/straight tendencies of all Eurocentric historiography" (169), Smith stands out in this collection for doing the difficult work of critiquing the very tendencies, terms, assumptions, and methods that make unsettling archival studies possible in the first place.

Part three, "Unsettling Praxis and Pedagogy: Toward Pluriversality," will be most useful to teacher-researchers interested in pedagogical applications of the theories and methodologies in classrooms. The approaches vary considerably among authors in this section. However, they have in common a commitment to enacting the priorities of critical archival studies and doing so in a fashion that mirrors the unsettling spirit of the collection. In chapter eleven, "Archival Imaginings of the Working-Class College Woman: The 1912-1913 Scrapbook of Josephine Gomon, University of Michigan College Student," Liz Rohan illustrates how a methodology of remixing might support Gilliland and Caswell's unsettling notion of "archival imaginings" (187), an approach that offers "enhanced understanding" and a more comprehensive historical record in cases where contents are not readily accessible or even missing. Rohan's approach is remarkable for its origins. Inspired by Jody Shipka and Jacqueline Jones Royster, she explains, ". . .my method is inspired by my students' projects in a first-year honors writing course in which I encourage creative writing as a method for scholarly inquiry" (188). Teacher-researchers seeking a detailed model of "archival imagining" that might function as a model for both research and pedagogy will find Rohan's contribution valuable.

In chapter twelve, Tarez Samra Graban's "Decolonizing the Transnational Collection: A Heuristic for Teaching Digital Archival Curation and Participation" offers readers a much-needed heuristic for ethical action in the contexts of transnational archives. Graban delineates a three-stage pedagogical approach in support of capacities meant to unsettle curatorial methods (218), temporality in service of the political diaspora of African women (221), and participation (225). She advocates for the characterization of archives as mobile spaces, "better traced" than "organized," and she offers a precondition for critical work that will appeal to critical archival studies practitioners: we must work to "delink the archive from specific regional expectations or geopolitical assumptions" (230). At stake, for Graban, is advancing the tacit promise of promoting "dialogic agility in decolonizing archival curation" (230). In chapter thirteen, "Archiving as Learning: Digital Archives as Heuristic for Transformative Undergraduate Education," Jennifer Almjeld fulfills a pedagogical promise of her own, presenting an account that will be convincing to readers who may be undecided about integrating archives into their teaching. She describes the creation of an undergraduate seminar, "Feminist Rhetorics," that coincided with the 2019 Feminism and Rhetorics Conference. In this seminar, students not only engaged with archives but also read scholarship to foster the development of "archival literacy" (as proposed by Jessica Enoch and Pamela VanHaitsma). In archiving with Almjeld, students actively created an archive for the conference. Almjeld shares important lessons learned in her conclusion. My favorite lesson, "It's Worth It," is a memorable reminder of the importance of critical archival studies in undergraduate education more broadly.

The final two chapters stand out as harbingers of the types of methodologies, research designs, pedagogical approaches, and outcomes that will result from more meaningful engagement with the lessons of this collection. In chapter fourteen, "Settling Emerging Scholars in Unsettling Territory: A Case Study of Underrepresented Students Working with Dominant Culture Collections," Rebecca Schneider and Deborah Hollis report on a case study documenting a course designed as an active-learning seminar focusing on archival research for students enrolled in the Miramontes Arts and Sciences Program (MASP) at the University of Colorado Boulder. Although the course structure provided undergraduates from underrepresented communities with chances to engage with advanced research methodologies and collaborate with archive staff, cultural differences and institutional and personal biases of archive staff negatively impacted some students' experiences. Schneider and Hollis thoughtfully frame and acknowledge the emotional stakes, anxiety, and pedagogical potential of these experiences. This chapter will be key to any instructor working with underrepresented communities and archives of dominant culture (276).

In the final chapter, "Unsettling Archival Pedagogy," Amy J. Lueck and Nadia Nasr reflect on their experience co-teaching a ten-week-long archival research course. The primary goal of this chapter is to center and theorize about unsettling moments students might encounter in performing research, or "students' limited positionality, discomfort, uncertainty, and other such unsettling moments" in the archival research process. Challenging "standard approaches to archival pedagogy" (285), Lueck and Nasr question the extent to which prevailing approaches account for the various ways "student research experiences are fundamentally implicated in ongoing histories of racism, sexism, and colonialism" (285). They describe how their own tendencies to resolve pedagogical tensions and "smooth the way" for student researchers "inadvertently allowed and even encouraged students to uncritically center themselves (and those like them)" (291). The authors' reflection invites readers weighing the pedagogical value of archival research to consider important questions:

> How could we go further in making silence, gaps, and intractable difference not simply a research inconvenience requiring other sources and source types? What if the limitations of our institutional archives weren't a liability or deficit in the rhetorical history classroom, but instead a lesson in themselves, spurring students to critical reflection on historical and ongoing inequity within the institution, and their own participation in those structures? What if the assignment was to identify and move *toward* those unsettling moments, those stumbling blocks, and to sit with them, recognizing

> their productive potential, rather than seeing them as the thing to avoid or work around? (295)

This collection is remarkable for its approach to addressing vexing, typically unresolved, and enduring social issues by offering lucid *yet* unsettled alternatives to key concepts (part one), methodologies (part two), and clear pedagogical paths and practical applications (part three). Readers of *Community Literacy Journal* will discover that this collection addresses a gap in ongoing discussions surrounding archival research in rhetoric and writing studies. In doing so, it offers new opportunities and perhaps alternatives to the idea of the "The Archival Wheel" as a starting point for meaning-making in archival research. It opens up the possibility of a heuristic with more dimensions—perhaps resembling a sphere with multiple centers—which might more completely acknowledge the haunted/ing complexities (13), wounded/ing spaces (6), and uncomfortable tensions inherent in bearing witness in our most unsettled moment.

Works Cited

Johnson, Nan. *Gender and Rhetorical Space in American Life: 1866–1910*. Southern Illinois UP, 2002.

—. "Autobiography of an Archivist." *Working in the Archives: Practical Research Methods for Rhetoric and Composition*. Eds. Alexis Ramsey, Wendy Sharer, Barb L'Eplattenier, and Lisa Mastrangelo. Southern Illinois UP, 2010: 290–300.

Searching for Literacy: The Social and Intellectual Origins of Literacy Studies

Harvey J. Graff. Palgrave Macmillan, 2022, pp. 314

Reviewed by Jamie D. I. Duncan
Lancaster University, Literacy Research Centre

"What is literacy studies? Where does it fit when we consider the cartography of academic disciplines? Does it develop out of sociolinguistics?" This is the broad shape of a few questions I heard during a seminar a few years ago. The graduate students who asked were keen to locate their discipline and their intellectual work. An eminent literacy studies scholar in the room replied sternly and tautologically that "literacy studies is literacy studies"—as opposed to reminding them of the field's rich interdisciplinary background. Yet, the students' questions are important exactly because of the field's interdisciplinarity. The broadness of literacy studies can lead to significantly different notions of the discipline's basic object and history. How do historians of literacy converse with elementary-level phonics teachers? In what departments do they work and do these departments cross-list their courses? Should they? Moreover, the more recent popularization of the concept 'literacies' has meant that it is not always clear what is being referred to by literacy or its pluralization. One of the central messages of Harvey Graff's new book *Searching for Literacy* is to go "back to basics" (3). These 'basics' he refers to and rethinks will probably be most familiar to researchers trained in New Literacy Studies (NLS) and 'literacy as a social practice' lineages—i.e., a conjoining of socio-culturally oriented interdisciplinary work on literacy in society that emerged through groundwork in the 1960s and 1970s, before becoming theoretically schematized in the 1980s. Alongside input from linguistics, anthropology, and psychology, Graff's work in history from the 1970s onwards was foundational to NLS. Graff apparently does not favor this 'new' moniker, yet central to the purposes of his book is an effort to "renew" approaches to literacy studies most closely associated with this research intersection (172). *Searching for Literacy* is an important and unique book, offering by far the most encompassing "Social and Intellectual Origins of Literacy Studies" both within this said purview and beyond it. The book is also much more forthrightly critical than previous disciplinary histories, with most of the founding scholars in the field receiving significant and at times abrasive critique. Numerous new frameworks are proposed that will prove useful for researchers. In short, this is a book that should be read by anyone with a stake in literacy studies research or an interest in literacy.

Chapter one introduces three points which underpin the book: literacy now, interdisciplinarity, and historicizing literacy studies. Graff begins by highlighting peculiar combinations of importance and ambiguity that notions of literacy have long retained in the "popular and political imagination" (3). What is literacy exactly, what is it for, and for whom? From social and critical theory to mainstream and corporate settings, expanding uses of this term 'literacies' is problematized likewise. Originally meant to situate varieties of literacy against acontextual and ahistorical understandings, Graff argues the term has lost theoretical and political meaning. Conceptual differences between multiple literacies and multiliteracies are addressed in the book, but these tend to be conflated in Graff's general criticisms of 'literacies.' Counter to increasingly metaphorical references to 'literacy' and 'literacies', Graff stresses that "definitions of literacy must be anchored in reading and writing across languages, symbol or sign systems, media, and domains of communication" (5). Renewed programmatic definitions of literacy based on this and related premises are forwarded throughout the book (5, 24). Epistemologically central here is an increased emphasis on *relationships* (e.g., semiotic, practical, historical)—differently, for example, to entrenched dichotomies (oral versus literate, illiterate versus literate, etc.), and to tendentially focusing on one mode over another (e.g., writing over reading). To what extent are speaking, reading, and writing researched in their relationships to each other? Graff suggests not as fully as they should be. Besides being a literacy studies scholar, Graff is an interdisciplinary scholar, offering theorizations on relationships across research fields. In chapter one he scales interdisciplinarity, from "disciplinary clusters (humanities, arts, social sciences, etc.)" to "dynamic interplay—critical and complementary—between disciplines (linguistics, anthropology, psychology, etc.)" (20). Further levels could be added here, but this viewpoint offers a useful relational and historicizing perspective. Whilst NLS is one example of an interdisciplinary research area, which Graff's historical work focuses upon, he argues neither NLS nor literacy studies have drawn sufficiently on theory and practice from history. Historical approaches forwarded through *Searching for Literacy* provide a corrective, "with more attention to a longer chronological span of intellectual and socio-cultural development" (15), where literacy is approached through a "multi-focal historical lens. . . mov[ing] between the wide angle and the close focus, the larger and the local" (15). Graff outlines key historical periods and processes in chapter one then expands in this same vein in subsequent chapters, namely chapter seven.

Chapters two through four focus on the main disciplines that have informed literacy studies according to Graff: linguistics, anthropology, and psychology. Although each chapter retains its respective disciplinary focus, significant interdisciplinary crossover in these chapters is noteworthy—where, for instance, linguistics necessitates discussion of anthropology, psychology, and history.

Chapter two focuses on linguistics and relationships between orality and writing through that discipline, which have informed literacy studies. Graff's criticism focuses on two main areas: first, insufficient theoretical and historical attention on the complexity of relationships between modes; second, long standing ideological dichotomies and their impacts. Graff summarizes these two interconnecting points as a "conundrum" (29). That is, where "the word . . . has long been said and written in different traditions and forms. But our knowledge of this—after the fact—necessarily comes through writing . . . [as well as] through centuries of translation and conflicting interpretations" (29). Graff affirms this set of relationships needs to be explored. However, he adds, "in the place of those relationships, we have a long legacy of formulaic divides surrounding [e.g.] 'from oral to written or literate' that also presume . . . an evolutionary trajectory" (29). Here readers are reminded of the primitive versus civilized binary consolidated through colonial-modernity, how this became framed later as a literate versus nonliterate binary, and how in turn educational-political institutions posited literacy's role in abstract-analytical thinking as a causal factor explaining 'developed' versus 'under-developed' economies and societies. Graff is rehearsing well-established criticisms in literacy studies here. However, he is arguing how these issues remain far from resolved, how they require attention in recontextualized and translated forms, and how doing so would connect contemporary concerns back to their social and intellectual foundations, and ground literacy studies disciplinarily.

One of Graff's corrective orientations is towards studies of orality. He argues most literacy studies have failed "to take orality seriously" (33), and even sociolinguists who do so, do not sufficiently emphasize "the dynamic and dialectical interactions between and among speech and writing (and other modes of literacy)" (33). These links Graff argues are fundamentally important for understanding the meaning and uses of literacy. It is interesting that he turns back to Ruth Finnegan—not regularly cited contemporarily in literacy studies, but an early pioneer of critical and expansive understandings of multimodality. Graff cites, but does not discuss directly, the more commonly referenced work on multimodality by Gunther Kress and colleagues. Finnegan is a classicist as well as an anthropologist, who specializes in oral literature amongst other areas. In this lineage Graff also draws attention to the seminal work of Milman Parry and Albert Lord and the oral foundations of Homer's *Odyssey*. These are rich sources for researchers to draw inspiration from—with examples that add complexity to notions of orality and literacy, and of composition, performance, and cultural transmission. More familiarly, Graff suggests that literacy researchers should look back more closely at Shirley Brice Heath's ethnographic research—e.g., beyond her conception of literacy events. He highlights an infrequently cited quote emphasizing orality, wherein Heath states: "examination of the contexts and uses of literacy in communities today may show that THERE ARE MORE LITERACY EVENTS WHICH CALL FOR APPROPRIATE KNOWLEDGE OF FORMS AND USES OF SPEECH EVENTS THAN THERE ARE ACTUALLY OCCASIONS FOR EXTENDED READING OR WRITING" (94, capitalization in the original). In the trajectory from Dell Hymes' and his colleagues' work on the ethnography of communication into the ethnography of literacy, Graff argues orality gets "all but lost" (54). Heath's work is held up as an exception.

Graff's focus in chapter three concerns anthropology and the anthropological turn in literacy studies, which is closely associated with the NLS. If this was a "turn" in literacy studies, Graff argues it was a "return" for anthropology. That is, although anthropologists such as Jack Goody, Brian Street, Shirley Brice Heath, and others framed anthropological approaches to literacy for late twentieth century researchers onwards, Graff reminds readers that understandings of literacy were central in founding anthropology as a discipline—from early modern distinctions between so-called primitive and civilized thought to much older archaeological-anthropological cross-cultural comparisons of writing systems and social systems. In short, Graff affirms in chapter three that while the influence of ethnographic approaches on literacy studies has been extensive, the broader disciplinary influence of anthropology has been insufficient. Through critically reengaging anthropology, and through rethought ethnographies of literacy that are more anthropologically ethnographic, literacy studies would consolidate and develop empirically and theoretically, according to Graff. As throughout the book, central to Graff's criticisms here are modernist and structuralist legacies of dichotomous thinking which remain prominent in literacy studies, where literacy remains, Graff claims, "a determinant of differences" (71). He apportions blame not only to Jack Goody and other "great divide theorists," who receive renewed criticism, but also to NLS researchers, particularly via influences of linguistics in anthropological and ethnographic literacy studies. The social anthropologist, Brian Street, Graff argues, is more interested in linguistics than sociology, economics, or history, for example. Graff does not mention both Goody and Street were English literature students prior to anthropology, which accounts for their continued interest in language. The suggestion is such ethnographic work on literacy would benefit from more emphasis on "complex human relationships" (74), and increased sophistication concerning "relationships" between literacy in theory and practice (72). Graff criticizes Street for his influential NLS distinction between "autonomous" and "ideological" models of literacy—i.e., another example of a binary division (albeit a didactic one) that drew attention away from how all models of literacy are ideological. For Graff, such foundational problems in the NLS reverberate through subsequent work. So, for instance, the premise of Deborah Brandt and Katie Clinton's well-known 'limits of the local' critique of Street and others' social practice perspective, itself falls into another false dichotomy. While acknowledging the age of the work, Barton and Hamilton's similarly influential "situated literacies" framework also receives criticism. Graff asks here "is it enough simply to say that literacy is 'situated' and that studies of literacy must be 'situated in context' without making more specific statements of a conceptual, comparative, and critical nature?" (94). Though scholars in this lineage might take issue that this suggestion is not already central to their thinking, Graff offers specific critique on each of Barton and Hamilton's axioms which will be useful for researchers drawing on this framework. In sum, while Graff's criticism is often harsh in this chapter, his motive is to move this work forward.

> The problem is conceptual and, even more fundamentally, epistemological. The crux of conceptualization pivots on the relational—dynamic, dialecti-

> cal, mutually reshaping, plural—oral *and* literate, texts *and* contexts, local *and* 'other' dimensions and origins . . . A renewed interest in the anthropology [and] ethnographies of literacy could focus more or less simultaneously on practices of reading and writing across media and on modes of understanding and communication across cultures, places, times, and other lines of differentiation and aim to develop theories of literacy based on those patterns of similarities and difference. Literacy—reading and writing as activities, not static attainments—would be conceptualized and studied as both theory and practice, in a dynamic relationship to each other. Such research would be parallel or at least systematically constructed, designed with collaboration and comparison in mind. (87–91)

In chapter four Graff addresses psychology. In one direction, he critiques cognitive psychologist David Olson's understanding of the "consequences of literacy" (building on Eric A. Havelock, Jack Goody, and others) (107–110). In another direction, Graff recalls attention to the cultural psychology of Sylvia Scribner, Michael Cole, and Barbara Rogoff as a way forward. Chapter four is extremely useful for researchers as a framework of discussion points and questions, which are practically applicable in a similar fashion to Barton and Hamilton's framework of literacy as social practice. Graff forwards these under the heading of "A Cultural and Social Psychology of Literacy" (123–127). Chapter four begins by historicizing psychology in philosophy, theology, and politics. This offers a counterpoint to popular, often ahistorical, representations of psychology in education as 'cutting edge' science (neuropsychology, etc.). Graff makes the trenchant observation that commonplace cognitivist versus culturalist debates will never be fully resolved, because "too many strong assumptions interfere with observations on subjects that typically are hard to study and harder to assess" (108). This is important for humanities and social science researchers working on literacy to remember in an increasingly high-tech world.

Chapter four continues with extensive criticisms of Olson's theories on "the impact of reading and writing—as a 'technology of the intellect'—on the mind or the brain" (107). This is a renewal of long-standing critique made by Graff, Finnegan, Street, and NLS scholars, amongst others. However, there is more depth and stronger criticism herein, alongside contemporary contextualization of these debates. "Have humans evolved from an oral to a literate and now to a digital mind? Is that a good or a bad thing? Of none of this is there direct or persuasive evidence" (109) affirms Graff, after fifty years of historical research on the topic. The basic idea of Olson and his colleagues' evolutionary theory of literacy and mind suggests that "the invention of the Greek alphabet and/or Western writing systems more generally led to changes in the human brain" (108). From there, a more complex argument is forwarded about how, put simply, meta-linguistic awareness resulted from literacy, and meta-cognitive awareness resulted in turn. This is, then, for them, a linear West-leading path, towards the abstract thinking, scientific advances, and social systemization of the modern world. Literacy is the building block. But all of this is deeply ahistorical for Graff, who asks, for example, "how do they know that preliterate or nonliterate people were incapable of reflecting on their own thought processes?" (110). In Olson's book *The World on Paper: The Conceptual and Cognitive Implications of Writing and Reading*, Graff points out that such basic historical questioning of "what world?" or "whose world?" is never really considered (Graff 113). Despite Olson's explanations of the development of Western "written culture," and a contemporary "literacy episteme," this research never accepts the argument that "practice is shaped, not by literacy by or in itself, but rather by institutions and the uses of literacy" (117). In response, Graff draws our attention back to Paulo Freire, Lev Vygotsky, cultural psychology, and other approaches that emphasize complex dialectical relationships. The cultural psychologist Barbara Rogoff summarizes this well where she lists: i) "literacy is an excellent example of the levels of relationship between the cognitive skills of the individual, the cultural technologies employed, and the societal institutions in which skill with technologies is practiced and developed", ii) ". . . variations in the purposes and practices of literacy appear to be closely related to the skills that individuals using a technology gain from its use," and iii) ". . . such variations are embedded in societal arrangements of human activities [which also change]" (Rogoff 54–55).

Chapter five covers literature and composition, but emphasizes reading. This emphasis is corrective. Graff argues literacy research has been disproportionately focused upon writing. Moreover, whether studying writing, or reading, or both, he claims there has not been sufficient focus on how these interrelate. Graff goes as far as to say that "the future of literacy studies, and of literacy, lies in the reconnection of reading and writing and their movement together" (152). Two of the book's programmatic points are forwarded in conjunction here, with Graff affirming "reading is the missing link in understanding, teaching, and practicing writing… [as] orality is the missing link in understanding literacy" (145). He suggests there has been a kind of writing fallacy in literacy studies, based on ideological models and practical ease. Together these lead to assumed understandings of reading which are incomplete. Graff reminds readers that "we know about and study reading through written records. In other words, writing provides the evidence of reading. That allows us to study what people read, but not how they did so and with what impact or influence" (146). Both this what and how are complex and at times contradictory. Graff discusses literary and historical work on, for example, the African American diaspora and English working classes, where writing and reading are central to processes of "social control *and* self-expression *and* self-determination" (149). Notice here the 'and' rather than 'versus.' Differently, Deborah Brandt's work on literacy and 'the rise of writing' in the U.S. is criticized by Graff for reinforcing unhelpful binaries. Brandt argues, for example, that there was a shift from an "eighteenth- and nineteenth-century era of 'mass reading literacy,' sponsored by church and state, [to] a more recent era of the ascendancy of 'mass writing literacy'" (151). It is this kind of explanation of literacy in history that Graff flags and interrogates throughout the book, where a non-dichotomous view and broader range of literatures and social histories would undo Brandt's too convenient distinction. Graff suggests a broader and more relational view helps us to contextualize, for instance, how commonplace rhetoric on the existence of a 'literacy crisis' and 'new' literacies associated with digital media have antecedents that go back centuries. He summarizes here that "a renewed understanding and appreciation of reading must move between typical studies of the availability of print or other reading material and ideologies in support of certain kinds of reading and censure of others, on the one hand, and actual practices, valuations, and influences of reading, on the other" (155).

Citing literary theorist John Guillory, Graff forwards two important concepts for reading in literacy studies—*translation* and *misreading*. The former concerns "the capacity of a reader to re-understand the world of a text by translating these words into a new frame of reference or intelligibility" (Guillory 9). The latter concerns how this ". . . process of interpretive reading is self-corrective and implies the necessity or inevitability or misreading or misinterpretation" (Guillory 9). Graff argues this kind of misreading is a key to reading development from school into university. Another conceptual framework forwarded in chapter five concerns "written culture" (a term used by Goody and Olson). Graff redefines three interlinking categories: deconstructing, re-conceptualizing, and reconstructing written culture (173–174).

> This approach means seeing written culture as historical and contradictory; as dynamic and developmental; as founded in reading and writing broadly construed; as constituted and conducted as oral and written; as collective and individual; as variable and based in both continuities and changes; and as constituted by contradictions and resistance, and conflicting structures of authority. (174)

Chapter six is titled "Many Literacies, Other Visions" and is the core of Graff's criticism. Yet, for me, it could have offered more clarity, especially from a disciplinary and theoretical perspective. The main problem it addresses has been discussed for over thirty years. That is, where the pluralized term 'literacies' becomes so broad it loses theoretical and political coherence. To understand how this occurred, a critical review of the differing uses and histories of the term seems fundamental, as occurs with other key terms in the book. Although Graff alludes to theoretical differences between multiple literacies, multiliteracies, literacy as metaphor, as analogy, and other related versions, he never really defines, differentiates, and historicizes these lineages. Consequently, when he talks about 'many literacies' in different ways, it is not always clear what he is referring to. To mention just one example, some work under the name 'health literacies' is based on theoretical approaches that emphasize reading and writing across modes and media. Elsewhere, references to 'health literacies' are found that have nothing to do with literacy or literacy practices at all—but Graff's critiques on such 'literacies' here in chapter seven, as elsewhere in the book, often seem to be conflated. It is helpful for researchers to understand the history of the concept of multiple literacies, for instance, in its development through, for example, the anthropology and sociolinguistics of language varieties, into literacy studies, and how this interacted with educational policy and identity politics from the mid-twentieth century onward. 'Multiple literacies' retention of fundamental notions of reading and writing in their relationships with other modes and practices involves significant differences to certain multiliteracies and multimodalities research. Recently, for example, one founding multimodality theorist suggested the NLS might be renamed New

Communications Studies (NCS)—that is, eradicating an assumed redundancy for the term literacy. Similar arguments have been made via recent work in the field of graphic pluralism. These approaches seem in conflict with Graff's mission of historicizing complex, relational, and recontextualized understandings of literacy and literacy studies.

Besides these criticisms, chapter six includes much useful material and important criticisms of the commercial appropriation of 'literacies.' Graff emphasizes the need for more historical and especially critical-theoretical work on digital literacies in literacy studies. To do so he suggests engaging more extensively with 'critical studies of digital media in cultural studies, media and journalism studies, and political economy' (197). From literacy studies, he highlights how 'great divide theories' and 'literacy myths' have been recontextualized through contemporary discourses on digital technologies. However, the main contribution of chapter six concerns another proposed framework, this time aimed at developing more cohesive comparative research on 'literacies' in literacy studies.

> One way of beginning . . . lies in identifying a small number of major forms of literacy that extend beyond traditional alphabetic literacy and may include some digital forms . . . In calling for their recognition, I argue for sustained study and exploration of their relationships to other forms of literacy. Herein lies the foundation for new, cross- and intermedial and modal forms of reading and writing, literally, metaphorically, and analogically. (202)

These five areas identified and defined in chapter six are visual, numerical, scientific, performance, and dance-movement literacies (203–215).

Next, in chapter seven Graff discusses history and he offers the caveat that all issues in the book have a "historical foundation: materially, epistemologically, and discursively" (227). As a rare academic that is both a historian and interdisciplinary scholar of literacy studies, Graff's advocacy of history for non-historians is important. History is a given in socio-cultural studies of literacy (e.g., via historical framings of 'context' relating to places, practices, and people). But this often seems intuitively done, rather than grounded in theory or literature on history. How many literacy researchers would be able to articulate methods, approaches, or concepts from the field of history? Many could do so via linguistics, anthropology, psychology, and education, among other areas. But why less so, I suspect, for history? Even in well-established research approaches such as Barton and Hamilton's literacy as social practice framework, Graff argues it is the historical component which is by far the least theorized. *Searching for Literacy* and especially chapter seven offer a wealth of material for development in this respect. "The history of literacy matters" begins Graff, but too often "dichotomies have substituted for relationships, assumptions for evidence and arguments" (227). In both direct and disguised ways, "literacy is linked to perceptions and expectations of change, when its experience is certainly as much associated with continuities" (227). The concept that Graff defines in most detail in chapter seven is "myth" (229–234). This is the foundation of his long-standing work on the "literacy myth . . . [i.e.] the belief, articulated in educational, civic, religious, and other settings, contemporary and historical, that the acquisition of literacy is a necessary precursor to and invariably results in economic development, democratic practice, cognitive enhancement, and upward social mobility" (229). His response to this ideology, deeply embedded within Western modernity, is that "only by grounding definitions of literacy in specific, contextualized, and historical particulars can we avoid conferring on literacy the status of myth" (230). In chapter seven, Graff gives an overview of the development of literacy in historical studies and more specific historical studies of literacy. Alongside 'relationships' another key word repeated here is 'complexity' in history, and how this can emerge through an awareness of historicity, whereby the "conceptualization, assumptions, and expectations we bring to considerations of reading and writing are revised radically when literacy is revisioned historically" (237), and in turn where "historical analysis and interpretation often have great power in stimulating fresh views, novel questions, and new understandings" (229). So, for instance, whilst multiple literacies, multilingualism, and visuality are frequently associated with twentieth and twenty-first century developments, Graff points to work on literacy in the middle-ages and renaissance that has much to teach us about these lineages. Graff offers an overview of work in historical literacy studies and explores a wide range of phenomena that sets up comparative frameworks with contemporary issues, from literacy's "relations with class, gender, age, and culture. . . [to] economic development, social order, mobility and stratification, education and schooling" (255). Graff asserts that "recognizing the history of literacy and its relevance to non-historians is at once a first step and a paradigmatic one" (260). He is correct. History in literacy studies can be approached in many ways, as this book illustrates, but whichever way, more significant engagement with history is fundamental.

Searching for Literacy is divided into two parts. Part one, chapters one through seven, end with an epilogue that brings together the main arguments of the book into a five-point pathway for a "revised, renewed literacy studies" (271)—one that is critical, comparative, and historical. These five pathways are headed as follows: i) Literacy and literacies are relational and dialectic; ii) Historical awareness is fundamental, iii) Context gives meaning to literacy and creates the ground for its study and practice, iv) Translation is inseparably intertwined with matters of literacy, v) Negotiation provides an especially human approach to the study and practice of literacy and literacies.

Pathways one through three will sound familiar to socio-culturally oriented literacy researchers, but Graff has suggested throughout the book that going back to basics as previously described is necessary. The foci of points four through five are the two interrelated concepts of 'translation' and 'negotiation' that Graff advocates for in chapter six. Translation is a historically and interdisciplinarily sensitive term which Graff argues "promotes learning from [a] wide range of theories," bringing together like terms, and reducing the need for neologisms (-trans-, -inter-, etc.) (273). Graff builds on Elizabeth Birr Moje and her colleagues' terminological development from 'hybridity' to 'navigation', but Graff argues that "the concept, theory, practice, metaphor, and notion of negotiation [are] more fitting, flexible, relational, and deeply human than notions of navigation or hybridity" (273). Translation and negotiation interlink as a research lens.

Following the epilogue, three short texts are appended as part two, chapters nine through eleven. Chapter nine summarizes and adds detail to ground covered in part one, concerning the development of the NLS in the 1970s, and what Graff considers the problematic proliferation of 'literacies' and resurgent 'literacy myths' evident contemporarily. Chapter eleven critiques in more detail 'financial literacy,' discussing a marketing campaign in the U.S. named FL4ALL "devoted to corporate profit-making" (293). Chapter ten is more innovative, addressing an issue of the utmost importance, and one both popular and scholarly audiences are seeking to understand. Graff discusses here what he terms "an unprecedented 'new illiteracy,' . . . [where] historical continuities are shattered by, first, the call to ban books in innumerable circumstances; second, the banning of written literature without taking the expected step of reading it; and, third, calls for not only banning but also burning books" (287). Together, he claims these constitute a kind of "a movement for illiteracy not a recognizable campaign for approved or selective uses of reading and writing" (287–288). Historical precedents of such bans and burnings stretch back from the 1960s U.S. civil rights movements to the sixteenth century reformation (to name just two). Graff notes a significant difference, however, where in these previous examples, actors "prided themselves on their direct familiarity with the explicit contents of that which they wished to ban (or even burn). They used their literacy in their brazen efforts to control the uses of others' literacy. Today's banners and burners, by contrast, are the new illiterates, achieving a rare historical distinction" (290). If there was ever a research topic that would benefit from the sophisticated approach to literacy studies that Graff lays out in *Searching for Literacy*, this seems it.

Works Cited

Guillory, John. "On the Presumption of Knowing How to Read." *ADE Bulletin*, 145, 2008, pp. 8–11.

Heath, Shirley Brice. *Ways with Words: Language, Life, and Work in Communities and Classrooms*. Cambridge University Press, 1983.

Rogoff, Barbara. *Apprenticeship in Thinking: Cognitive Development in Social Context.* Oxford University Press, 1990.

Coda

Editors' Introduction

As our own act of radical imagination, we, as an editorial collective, rethink our role in disrupting silence given the violent realities in Gaza. As we discussed and studied the pieces in this issue, we heard, saw, and felt more clearly how they disrupt the status quo and illustrate the possibilities of Coda as a space for rhetorical disruption and creative practice. The phrase silence = death was coined during the AIDS epidemic of the 1980s. Today, silence = death among marginalized queer communities, in racist societies, and in systems of pervasive rhetorical violence. Today, silence = death in Gaza.

One cause of silence around the violence in Gaza is the either/or framing that identifies only two positions: pro-Israel or anti-Jewish. This either/or framing is a form of intellectual bullying that conceals the possibility of finding common ground and perpetuates colonial ideologies that remove Palestine and the Palestinian people from the conversation, obscuring their suffering and needs. Today, silence = death in Gaza.

As a team of editors from various layered identities and backgrounds, which include Jewish, Palestinian, and white American, we want to make a space to move beyond these harmful dichotomies; to look instead at lived realities; and to call upon our friends and colleagues to do the same. Coda aims to continue a historical tradition that makes space for critical and creative voices and visions that are often silenced in conventional academic conversations. As such, we aim to continuously consider the ethical complexity of this work. By publishing pieces in a range of modalities and genres (in this issue alone, we feature poetry, experimental theater, non-fiction, quilting, list-making, and a graphic essay), we hope to challenge dichotomies that narrow what counts as knowledge.

Because narrow genre conventions in academic spaces often perpetuate silence, we found ourselves thinking about the other ways that the systems mediating our lives silence us. We thought about the idea of radical imagination and whether it's even possible when our lives are enmeshed in systems rooted in racist, colonial histories that function to benefit people already in power. Reckoning with the violence in Gaza reminded us of the ambient precarity that ensues from these systems. We considered the subtle and overt forms of control that keep us from building a more just world, and we asked how we might better come in solidarity from different standpoints in the face of individual and collective fears.

As we worked with the authors featured in this issue, we learned that radical imagination is possible when we find the collective support needed to disrupt the passive silence and fear that maintains rigid societal structures. The pieces in this special issue of Coda exemplify radical imagination as they break passive silence to make noise meaningful. As with every issue of Coda, we seek to make space for Audre Lorde's call to "transform silence into language and action."

We open with poetry that locates and lives in the excitement and caution of community building, respectively. The poem "First Pride Parade in My City" by Saurabh Anand preserves the first pride parade in the speaker's city as a significant moment of rhetorical action. Through sonic and visual elements, the poem conveys the enduring, expanding effects of the community coming together for this occasion. The poem documents the significance of the speaker's participation in this community event outside, yet as an extension of his academic work. Then, Mara Lee Grayson highlights the problematic limitations of academic spaces. In three poems, she locates the discomfort of working in and with a "not-exactly-chosen community." Grayson reflects on the hypocrisies of institutions of higher education where faculty and administrators speak about progress while the institution perpetuates the status quo.

Other authors in this section reimagine genres from status quo formats to make space for more creative and critical work. Working from field notes, Sarah Puett builds a narrative essay, "Institutional Departure," from her time with a racial justice organization in the Twin Cities. She compiles and reflects on her experiences as a sometimes-participant and sometimes-observer during these gatherings, and conveys the complexities of belonging and contributing in activist spaces.

In Tracey Bullington's "Gratitude," illustrated characters swap moments of gratitude over email, thankful for a favorite flavor of ice cream and a fixed flat tire. This daily exchange is imagined literally and textually through the form of a graphic essay. Using other familiar forms, Evan Harris illustrates an imagined—but also real—invitation to Pros & Cons list-makers to share their lists of decision-making. Playing with the rigidity and norms of a call for presentations, Harris helps us ask questions about what a virtual community can be and how that community might start from a QR code. Perhaps the call is an invitation for us to consider how any text on a page always exceeds that page, the journal that holds it, and the time of its publication.

We end this section with two experimental works: a play excerpt and the documentation of a community quilting project. In "A Meta-staging of the Initial Investigative Operatics Working Group, With [x number of] Original Cast Members Playing All the Parts," Bethany Ides, Fan Wu, Ora Ferdman, and Zoe Tuck use multiple and shifting speakers, modes, and forms to position the reader as an active participant in complex inquiries that flirt with the absurd as much as the serious. Then, "Against Forgetting: Quilt Pieces and Reflection," Susan Naomi Bernstein's project, offers a material, poetic, and rhetorical testimony to the power of community writing to sustain contestatory positions and kinesthetic knowledge "stitch by neverending stitch." Through photography and writing, this piece stitches together quilt-making, poetry, and Zoom community gatherings, creating a multimedia argument for work that echoes beyond the page.

We call upon ourselves and you, our readers and writers, to join us in committing to the liberatory potentials of our work, to use our positions to push back against violent silence and violence, to seek out accurate information about the crisis in Gaza, and to bring these commitments to our community work. As much as we aspire for Coda to be a space for the preservation of projects such as those in this issue that move us beyond the dualities that contribute to violence, such as the violence in Gaza today, we have realized that we need to slow down and learn more so that we can fulfill these aspirations without doing harm. For this reason, we are taking a pause from soliciting new work to study antiracist, decolonial, and anti-ableist editing practices, to reflect on our own positionalities, and to build better systems and practices. We expect to share a CFP for the spring 2025 issue early next fall. In the meantime, we invite you to stay in touch with us, especially if you have feedback for us or suggestions for texts we might study or people we might listen to.

Thank you,
The Coda Editorial Collective.

First Pride Parade in My City

Saurabh Anand

Reflection

As an educator and a queer resident-of-color of Athens-Clarke County and Georgia, I often join my colleagues in knocking on the doors of local and state government organizations to show our collective dissent when diversity or diverse thoughts were in danger and demanded support for minorities to thrive, live on their term, and feel safe in the city we lovingly call Athens. This piece is my poetic storytelling of the first Pride Parade organized in 2022 by Athens Pride and Queer Collective (see Rymarev, 2022), a local queer organization, and the installation of rainbow crosswalks downtown that acknowledges and uplifts queer voices in the city. I see pride parades as an essential community-building exercise that bridges and represents local community members' diverse histories, leading to a broader purpose and meaning-making of their living experiences. Through my thoughts in this poem, I intrinsically argue the importance and inevitable connections of communal equality and equity endeavors as parts of pedagogy and andragogy.

Contributing to such ongoing participation in my city, I show my commitment as a queer educator to community partnership initiatives and the relevance of the strong connections between what happens outside my classroom, such as at home or with family or in other social places, and their connections inside my classroom. This poem is a small step in showing how storytelling legitimizes queer experiences I teach and hear within and beyond my educator's and/or queer individual capacities.

Work Cited

Rymarev, E. (2022, June 13). Athens hosts first annual pride parade. *The Red & Black*.

First Pride Parade in My City

June 12.
Athens' noon. Close to 100 degrees, yet hearts were over the moon.

Because,
that day, the matter all gathered for, and the cascades of the past that we all use to contemplate mushroomed - bloomed into the Pride victory - to celebrate us, our histories.

Voices,
which were sadly getting used to being shunned, drummed, the band of their throne.
Through sincere deliberations, we sow "atypical" foundations. Love prevails across bridges,
forms, and colors. I saw a toddler and her mothers sharing happy kisses. Pride in air and hearts.

Cheered,
Seeing the crowd, pals in college gear, my heart nudged me to teach about
our city's better reach. Athens' Clayton Street or College Ave are not just routes -
they house people's rights, gotten after long fights. They're the sites where all-of-kind love resides, taking Athens to a better societal height. Our city is now a better place, y'all. Plumb!

Author Bio

Saurabh Anand is a rhetoric and composition PhD student and an assistant writing center director in the Department of English at the University of Georgia. *The English Journal, The Autoethnographer*, the *Washington Square Review, the Journal of Writing and Writing Courses*, and the *South Florida Poetry Journal* featured his creative works.

Three Poems

Mara Lee Grayson

Reflection: On the Significance of Writer Friends

Over the last two years, as legislation and sociopolitical white supremacist bullshit have decimated antiracist curricula and other efforts toward educational equity, as I've been disappointed by supposedly progressive universities that don't protect students or employees (see Nguyen), and as colleagues I admire have left the academic workforce, I've been thinking about irony. There's a special irony in how academia allows itself to be weaponized, its faculty and students sacrificed to the status quo. Knowledge production has outpaced institutional progress, and academic institutions continually pull us back to status quo operations that ignore everything we know from the scholarship we produce, everything institutional leaders should have learned in recent years. Students aren't the only ones who suffer when capitalistic, ethnocentric, ableist notions of normality and success are shoved down our throats.

We forget that we are always in a not-exactly-chosen community, for better or worse, with peers and colleagues. Too many of us suffer, if not at the hands of deliberately cruel or self-serving people, then because of the whitely whims and neoliberal motivations of toxic departments and universities that seek to fortify their gates. Like other multiply-marginalized scholars, I've written about experiences with ostracism and discrimination that (not so) coincidentally began when I challenged institutional whiteness (Grayson). I've been subjected to sexist, antisemitic, and ableist attitudes, coded into criticisms of my voice, demeanor, hometown, and politics. I've navigated retaliation, runaround, and betrayal by colleagues I thought were allies. Unsure how to express what I've felt in scholarly discourse – or even sometimes in full sentences – I began writing and publishing poetry again. I also returned to teaching creative writing.

My fall 2022 creative writing class met in a room too small for 25 people during a public health crisis. Wearing masks, students wrote, shared, and revised; I did the same at home. I emphasized expression and connection and encouraged codemeshing. I shared Melissa Febos's celebration of personal essay as social justice work: "The only way to make room is to drag all our stories into that room. That's how it gets bigger" (28). A poet friend from my MFA days gave a reading and we talked about the importance of writer friends to trust with shitty first drafts. Students discussed their experiences with life as well as language: one read a genre-defying reflection upon the loneliness of dorming on a predominantly commuter campus; he added that making a friend in class had been the high point of his semester. Another read a personal essay about being sexually assaulted in high school. Her peers thanked her for trusting them with her story. It felt good to share, she said.

"This was really a life class," one student told me at the end of the semester. On evaluations, alongside positive comments about my teaching, students critiqued the classroom's unsuitability as a space for sharing creative writing. They distinguished between my teaching and the institutional context forced upon us and used the evaluation to voice their concerns. Though mistreatment had made me question my role in the institution, I'm not sure I've ever felt as successful as an educator.

That success resulted not from particularly brilliant teaching or even an especially brave cohort of student writers but instead from a confluence of factors in that place and time, one of which was the writing we shared. Though all writing may enable writers to retell trauma stories from positions of agency, personal essay and poetry may allow writers to (re)present and reconfigure experiences of trauma, which most human beings have experienced (Boysen). Through poetry, we can put language to the intensity and nonlinearity of our emotions and cognition. Through personal essay, we may (re)claim and find audiences for our stories.

I realize now that what disappoints me isn't that institutions keep resorting to the status quo. Institutions will institution. What disappoints me is how many colleagues, how many of *us*, not only let it happen, but adjust our behavior accordingly, bolster the institution, and throw each other under the bus. We can learn a lot from our students about supporting each other, not just as scholars but as people. Writing has helped me connect with parts of myself I let lie dormant, and it helped me connect with students during a difficult time in many of our lives. It has reminded me, too, of the importance of writer friends: When we share our language and stories with each other, we offer readers something of ourselves and the world as we live it, whether our language takes the form of poetry, personal essay, or scholarship. Good readers honor that responsibility.

When it comes to scholarship, I've taken on as many collaborative writing projects as I have solo-authored ones in recent years. I've made new writer friends.

References

Boysen, Guy A. "Evidence-based Answers to Questions about Trigger Warnings for Clinically-based Distress: A Review for Teachers. *Scholarship of Teaching and Learning in Psychology,* vol. 3, no. 2, pp. 163-177, 2017.

Febos, Melissa. *Body Work: The Radical Power of Personal Narrative.* Catapult, 2022.

Grayson, Mara Lee. "Antiracism is Not an Action Item: Boutique Activist and Academic (anti)Racism." *Writers: Craft and Context,* vol. 3, no. 1, pp. 65-74, 2022.

Nguyen, Alexander. "Audit Exposes Flaws in Cal State University's Handling of Sexual Assault Cases." KPBS. May 26, 2023. https://www.kpbs.org/news/education/2023/05/26/audit-exposes-flaws-in-cal-state-universitys-handling-of-sexual-assault-cases

The Palm Tree is Not Indigenous to Southern California: A Poem for Our Colleagues Who Are Too Busy Reading White Fragility *to Actually Do Anything about Racism*

Professor, maybe I don't have the history
to handle all the dissonance I've learned
defines the woman's wonder at the west.

The palm trees missionaries planted
have borne centuries of gossip,
and I'm getting tired of trying

to clarify: Some roots are shallow,
fibrous, herbs we've misidentified;
self-accountability requires growth,

not absolution; and language matters
more to one whose tongue is branded
foreign. Irony is lost to fear

emboldened by fragility, while they teach us
to ignore the inspiration
seeping from the fading sun. Grit grows

wide as hope, but palms still stand
like mysteries of villages
burned up and abandoned long ago:

Yes, germ can be both seed and byproduct.
No wonder now I dream
in meter: Drums beat in my ears

to keep me marching
in the night, while travelers lose track
of what is fiction, what is magic,

and empty out the building,
inviting rumors to proliferate
then occupy each unmade bed.

Migrant butterflies are buried
in the pavement, fossilizing fast
beneath this clusterfuck

of fertilizer and debris
that calls itself a university: Sometimes
I wish it all burnt to the ground,

but what would it become?
Just another plot in which to plant
another stubborn patch of palm trees.

Weather Report

You can't control the narrative that's used
against you when your voice is stuck
                                        inside a shell that spins
and spirals. Winds, tornadoes, hurricanes
can cause the ears to ring and block the sound
a counterstory makes.

                                        I'd tell it plain
if I could only:

                                        Once there was a storm
that drowned a city, first the east and then
the west. You learned to swim. And then there was
an ocean, all was water, there were sharks,
a ship that pounded waves. You can't outswim
its wake; the wake is all the voice you've left.

A storyteller's slant: You made the choice
to sail with sharks on ships disguised as prey.

The Director's Daughter

I used to be a method actor, which means
I never lied. I learned to play both parts

of any given dialogue when everyone was busy
being someone else. I was, meanwhile,

aligned with expectations, typecast
as the naïve perpetrator: Eve impaled

by the serpent's fang. Once upon a time,
everybody knew my father. Then,

a cigarette I write into my character, high
school black box smoke alarm deactivated.

An airplane bottle, bourbon in the library
before I get onstage to cry.

Pretending long enough a kiss is real
to make it so. It was a different time,

says one of me; the other's sure it wasn't.
If I hurt you, I believed I wasn't me that time.

Now I'm haunted by my father's face
when I look in the mirror. I saw flashes

of our futures, but how could I predict
their order? A quiet audience won't care

if sea or salt came first or if once we were
inseparable, contents and containers,

and soon will be again. Then the boat adrift:
I was a dreamer in the water,

while you treaded for time. I floated
on a lover's belly, buoyed by his ebb and sigh.

I thought myself to sleep each night,
the performer all alone onstage, yet so

distractable, telling truth but out of turn.
You should have known my head would spin

a story that my mouth refused
to wrap itself around. I'll meet whatever mark

you want, and call myself by any name,
if you'll let my lips make seven words

in shape: I was here, and I hurt too.

Author Bio

Mara Lee Grayson's books include *Teaching Racial Literacy: Reflective Practices for Critical Writing*, *Race Talk in the Age of the Trigger Warning: Recognizing and Challenging Classroom Cultures of Silence*, and *Antisemitism and the White Supremacist Imaginary: Conflations and Contradictions in Composition and Rhetoric*. Her poetry has been nominated for fancy awards but hasn't won any of them. Previously a tenured faculty member, she currently works as the Director of Content Development for the Campus Climate Initiative at Hillel International.

Institutional Departure

Sarah Puett

Reflection

In the fall of 2016, I participated with a local racial justice organization in the Twin Cities, TCO (Twin Cities Organizing), by contributing to a campaign for creating alternative means to public safety. I attended meetings, generated ideas, canvassed, did a lot of listening, and later wrote about some of the meetings as part of my dissertation, which considered the relationship between critical literacy and activism in the public sphere. The following selection is a collection of "written up" fieldnotes—meaning I typed out my hand-written self-notes and added in detail, reflection, and context for an audience. The idea was to raise questions rather than offer cogent answers about the role negotiation that is involved in community literacy projects and in doing rhetorical fieldwork, which was considered an "emergent" practice at the time. In some ways, I want to push back on the idea that field methods in literacy and rhetorical studies are emergent; they have a long, storied, and checkered history. I recognize the value of some of the more established, typical lines of study one could pursue with fieldnotes "data," e.g. as study of multimodality or embodiment, participatory composition or geocomposition, or an examination of community-led resistance movements. All of these are productive lines of inquiry.

When my methods took me outside and away from the academy, I learned about the *emergency of community*. My experience highlighted the temporal urgency of being together, of radical hospitality, and of the importance of collective unlearning. I came to see, over the course of a year of participatory fieldwork, that my notions of "community literacy" were misguided. Community literacy isn't something I know about because of what academic literature tells me. Community literacy is something that lives—something cultivated through a series of experiences with others, over an extended period, through sustained participation and mindful observation, motivated by an ethic of care. In part, this work illustrates my rejection of the dissertation as a primarily academic genre or an *act of social removal*, as Richard Rodriguez puts it. My project is inherently social. It was informed by local events, personal relationships, national conversations, and my reading of the sociopolitical landscape. I hope this work also stands as a testament to the vast project of critical literacy and the processes of both learning and unlearning that an emancipatory project requires.

Institutional Departure

September 2016

I couldn't figure out what to do.

I pulled off my sunglasses and looked up at the towering structure before me, wondering if I'd gone to the wrong place. The door was locked. But I'd confirmed the address with Remy that same morning. It had turned into one of those unreasonably and unseasonably hot September afternoons, the kind that belonged back in August. I could feel sweat gathering on my hairline.

"You need in here?" While I was peering upward an older man stepped out of the shop next door. "Oh hi, yeah, is this the door, or…?" I was glad to see someone. "Yea, it is, this place always confuses people," he said as he rapped a few times on the glass door. He seemed like he'd done this before. He was peering through the front of the building, watching for movement, saying something about how the lights appeared to be off. I stepped forward to look with him. We exhaled in unison when we noticed a woman heading towards the door. I thanked the man for his help. As he brought a cigarette to his mouth, he nodded his head and squeezed his eyes shut for a moment, the way some people do when accepting a compliment, and stepped back towards his shop. Was it his shop? I kind of wanted to have a smoke with him so I could ask, but I was fully sweating by then. I was ready to go inside.

"Hi, I'm Sarah, I have a meeting with Remy?" I blared when she opened the door. I still wonder if I said it as loud as my memory tells me I did. I still wish I could remember what she said in return. I still wonder why I never saw her again after that day. I had loudly stated my purpose, and the man with the smokes had knocked loudly on the plate glass, and meanwhile, inside, about fifteen organizers sat quietly together, heads bowed, in a healing circle. There were candles and soft music. *Fuck*, I thought, *I definitely interrupted*. My shoulders fell as the woman escorted me through the room. Remy jumped up from working on his laptop as soon as he saw us coming. I apologized for being a little early, and for interrupting. He explained that healing circles were common at Twin Cities Organizing (TCO) and necessary for organizers working on the front lines of social justice activism. "We're all just trying to make sense of the brutality and chaos that the last week has been," he said, circling his index finger in the air like a whirlwind.

I didn't ask exactly what he meant because I felt like I knew. I wonder what he would have said. I guess I learned something about asking good questions somewhere along the way. Earlier that week 43-year-old Keith Lamont Scott was fatally shot by police in Charlotte, NC. Minutes afterward, Scott's daughter recounted what happened using Facebook Live: "They shot my daddy 'cause he's Black. He was sitting in his car reading a mother fucking book. So they shot him. That's what happened." The national news media didn't put it that way of course, and despite playing the video over and over again, most of the mainstream media seemed to ignore her perspective entirely. CNN kept bringing up a car crash that left Scott mentally impaired, and kept saying it was "unclear" whether or not Scott had a gun, and kept bringing up the Blackness of the police officer who shot Scott. Later they honed in on the protests, where civilians were killed, and others were injured. Remy might've referenced all or none of this if I'd asked what he meant or what the week had been like for him. It didn't feel appropriate to open with trauma.

State sanctioned violence against Black Americans felt far too ordinary, feelings of outrage felt far too familiar, and media coverage proved that as a country we were far short of a collective story about what was happening and why. Remy might've said something like that. He might've said something about what he, as a young Black man, was experiencing, that a young white woman couldn't understand. Should I have asked? Should I have called attention to a disparity in our grief? What was the disparity exactly? Disrupting the healing circle had made me feel rude and invasive, and I didn't want to make a worse impression by seeming out of touch. There's often no right answer in situations like this, so I tried to just stay present and in the moment. Comfort is too often a tool of white supremacy.

Sometime after I interrupted the healing circle that day at TCO, I thought back to a moment when I learned about the disparity of grief. I was at a BLM protest that took place shortly after Freddie Gray was killed by Baltimore police in the spring of 2015 (see Figure 1). That evening a young Black organizer looked out over a crowd of more than a thousand Minnesotans gathered in Gold Medal Park and called attention to the number of white folks in the crowd. She asked all people of color to come to the top of the hill where she spoke through a megaphone. She explained that the pain and fear people of color were experiencing needed to be made central in that moment. I'm not sure I'd heard anyone in Minnesota say something so honest or so necessary (the passive aggression in Minnesota is too real). She asked all the white allies to stay back, to move down the hill, and to be quiet, while people of color embraced one another, sang, and swayed in the sun. That experience shaped my role as an accomplice because it taught me about shared and unshared grief, emotional labor, and #whitefolkwork.

That first meeting at TCO, the doors were open to each of the offices that lined a brightly lit room with two large tables at the center. The table-top and the walls were completely covered with posters, drawings, writing, banners, colors, photos, notes, and other writing, from the floor to the ceiling. The space, Remy said, was a good way to tell the story of TCO, an activist group formed in 2010 by organizers who met while working on local issues related to #OccupyWallstreet. I noticed some #Occupy tokens on the walls. I've always loved writing and I particularly love writing-rich environments—from personal inspiration boards to community bulletin boards. I thought about all the different tools that had been used to create those materials. Some of it was done in colored pencil, some marker, some of it was printed, a great deal of it was handwritten. It was so colorful and loud. Remy and I stood there and marveled at it together for a few minutes. Looking back, I wonder less about the tools and more about the people who made all those materials and where they all ended up, especially after TCO shut down.

Figure 1. Photo of BLM protest in Minneapolis, MN, April 2015. This photo shows a large gathering of diverse people on a green hilltop with blue sky in the background. On the right someone holds up a large handwritten sign that says BLACK LIVES MATTER, while at the top of the hill stands an organizer speaking into a megaphone.

TCO had recently moved into this building after a fire destroyed their old office down the block. The fire raged for over three hours, taking out local businesses and apartments as well as the historic buildings that housed them. Only four injuries were reported, but eleven apartments were burned up and twenty-three people lost all their belongings. TCO organizers led a thousand-person march for higher minimum wage that morning, but by that afternoon they launched a fundraiser for those affected by the fire. In the end they raised and distributed over $20,000 to residents displaced by the fire, and with the help of the grassroots community and a few prominent citizens, they raised enough funds to purchase the lot where their office had been. They planned to rebuild. But after investigators revealed that arson was the probable cause of the fire, negotiations fell through. "We raised all the money, but in the end the owner wouldn't let us build," Remy told me, with despair and irritation.

Remy and I both talk absurdly fast, so talking came easy. At the time I didn't know one-to-one meetings were a recurrent form of labor for organizers like him, but it makes sense looking back. It's the same for us writing teachers. He was used to talking about TCO to a variety of audiences. As we settled into chairs on either side of a wooden desk, I asked him about the momentum I was noticing. I'd seen TCO's name all over the place that summer. "Yea, there's a bunch of reasons," Remy said, as a laundry list seemed to populate in a thought bubble above his head. "The conversations we're leveraging" was the one that seemed the most important, but he also said the organization's hybrid model, their physical space, and their leadership were all reasons for their success. TCO is made up of 95% Black leadership, out of 20 full-time employees, all of whom are from the Twin Cities. "We've had consultants come in from outside, but otherwise we're completely local."

With membership numbers in the thousands (local and non-local), members pay dues, attend meetings, and vote on campaigns driven by local issues, particularly for those living in under-resourced communities and communities of color. "We leverage people power," Remy told me. "We're willing to work with-*in* and with-*out* the system… We aren't afraid to shut down a city council meeting or walk on a freeway, but we are really interested in policy change." He told me about the policy that resulted from their campaign for paid sick leave as an example: "150,000 people's lives will change for the better once that policy takes effect." He said TCO interns analyze campaigns like that one from start to finish during their training: "From the moment a member brings an issue to the table to the moment a policy takes effect." I was eager to hear more about those trainings. I was eager to hear more about everything TCO was doing. I was especially interested in their new campaign on police accountability. "We decided to sit down and think about how we can stop paying the police force thousands of dollars a year to kill us." *I'm in,* I thought. I later learned that, in fact, the Minneapolis Police Department had an annual budget of $160 million.

October 2016

My memory tells me there were over 100 people in the room that day. TCO was packed. I wanted to get some pizza but couldn't see it from where I was sitting. I didn't want to lose my seat, so I didn't get any. As I was craning my neck to lay eyes on the pizza, I noticed some of the relics from the bank that previously occupied TCO's space. There was a recognizable main desk area, some teller windows, and a big open floor where people probably used to form lines. What an institutional departure. I'd been meagerly talking to a woman sitting next to me who taught at a school on the Northside, where a friend of mine did her student teaching. She said it was her first time at TCO. Did I bring up the bank relics to her? I can't remember. I know I was thinking it, but I'm not sure I voiced it… Slap some vivid green paint on the walls, pepper in some groovy local art, pack the space with folks who want to speak truth to power… Radical change can happen anywhere. But, as I later learned, I shouldn't have assumed everyone was there for the same reason. This was the first meeting for the police accountability campaign that Remy told me about a few weeks earlier. The public event description on Facebook read as follows:

> It's more and more clear every day – our current model of 'public safety' is simply not keeping us safe. With every death we mourn – Philando Castile, Jamar Clark, Korryn Gaines, Tyre King, Terrence Crutcher, Keith Lamont Scott – we know that it's time to envision a world without punitive and antiquated models of law enforcement. We must begin to build and resource radical new public safety alternatives to police.

I was there because I knew that to be true, but I didn't quite know what to do about speaking truth to power. I wanted to get more involved in racial justice work because I was upset, pissed off, confused, disillusioned with academia, and wanted to participate in my community. I was starting to understand that I needed to be doing local *anti*-racist work on-the-reg. And evidently, I wasn't the only one. The room was full of white people.

Amara, one of the TCO organizers, quieted the group and thanked everyone for coming. She asked that we begin by sharing our preferred pronouns. Then Amara (she/her) introduced another young Black woman named Tanya (she/her). Before Tanya said anything, I remember thinking she didn't look comfortable. Her gaze was cast downward. Over the next several minutes Tanya told us a story about when she called the local police department to help her resolve a domestic dispute, and the officers who showed up shot her. Twice. In her house. In front of her family. I'll never forget the way she motioned in towards her stomach with her two fingers to show how the bullets went in. The way she gestured, that's how it felt to her. She didn't speak very loudly, she wasn't up there for very long, and she looked down the entire time. She said things didn't have to go down the way that they did, and she wished they hadn't. She showed us with her body that we need alternative means for public and community safety. She wasn't a story we were reading about in the news, she wasn't a statistic we were trying to understand, she was a person – alive and real, standing in front of a bunch of strangers, telling us about how her life could have ended. While my whiteness had insulated me from a number of traumas, there was nowhere to hide at that moment. I remember anxiously wondering if anyone would clap when she finished speaking. Her bravery deserved applause, certainly, but one wouldn't want to confuse what we were clapping about. Instead, the room was so silent it screamed.

"Enough is enough," Remy said as he took the floor. "It's time for us to start talking about taking these systems back and making sure the policing system we have is dismantled." He told us how the first formal slave patrol was established in 1704 in South Carolina, where armed militia were ordered to apprehend and punish any African Americans caught without documentation from wealthy, white, plantation-owning men. While the first police department was established in Boston in 1838, slave patrols were already institutionalized by then, and the Fugitive Slave Act of 1850 further established the patrol's use of force. Remy mentioned that some referred to the 1850 Act as the Bloodhound Law because of the dogs that were used to "hunt" runaway slaves. When he began walking through the relationship between slave patrol tactics and tactics used by the modern police force, I wondered what the modern equivalent was for the dogs.

Before splitting us into groups, Remy also talked about alternatives to public safety, referencing community policing models being piloted in areas of Chicago and New York. The goal was to discuss alternative visions to safety in our community and solutions for decreasing police intervention. We needed to use our imaginations, to share our most creative ideas, and to consider "Step Up/Step Back." Remy described this as a model for discussion where people who usually speak up take a step back, and those who usually don't, step up. People of color were to speak first and ahead of white people in every breakout, each of which was facilitated by a Black organizer.

When we came back together as a group we reported out some of our conversation pieces while TCO organizers wrote them by hand on big pieces of paper with adhesive on the top. I liked that they stuck wherever you wanted to put them, and I love the way handwritten ideas look on a wall (see Figure 2).

Figure 2. Photo of the writing on the wall. This photo shows a group of people sitting in chairs facing three presenters and a large neon green wall with large pieces of paper on them; the paper has handwriting on it that is unreadable from this vantage point.

November 2016

There were a lot of people at TCO that I'd never seen before that night. It was just a few days after the 2016 Presidential election. I noticed a white kid standing up in the middle of the room with his arms crossed. He seemed to be about 18 years old, which I guess I determined based on his hoodie, his acne, and his general demeanor. The meeting was starting, but the room never got all the way quiet. The place was tense. The organizers began to describe the new campaign for resistance, which would be exclusively led by people of color. Suddenly, all the eyes in the room darted to a white guy who'd begun to yell: "Why is this organization led exclusively by people of color?" The way he asked the question did not feel friendly. Everyone stirred, weight shifted, wounds opened, and all manner of things began to spill out into the room. Soon the microphone made its way into the hands of Drake, who was arguably the charismatic leader of the organization despite its decentralized model. I'll never forget the look of patience on his face.

He said that TCO's Black organizers—and the experience of Black Americans in general—were uniquely suited for the current political moment. He talked about how the lived experiences and the history of racial oppression uniquely prepares Black Americans to inform the present political moment and guide the political movement for racial justice. He said something along the lines of what he said later in an interview, whose transcript I can no longer find:

> We're on the Northside on a cold Wednesday, a room full of people talking about race, class, resistance. My sense is this is happening all over the country, all over the country there are rooms just like this. People are wrestling with this, wanting to resist, and that's tremendously hopeful… There is a mass resistance all over the country and there is an element of joy. When I talk to people there's fear, but there is an optimism, and a big middle-finger fuck you, we're going to do it our way. A lot of that is coming from youth and folks of color, and can we bring that to rural America? It's an amazing opportunity... This is a country where an abolitionist movement fundamentally wrestled with *whether or not I'm a human being*. This is nothing compared to some of the social movements that we've been through in this country. We've pushed through, we've created a better country. This is no different than that. In fact it's probably less daunting that a lot of the other moments we've been in and there's a major, major opportunity to re-shape and re-wire the country if we seize the moment and don't shy away from it.

Some white people had some feelings about this. I don't remember exactly what they said, and I wouldn't recount it even if I did, but I do remember thinking that this wasn't the best use of our time. Couldn't these people ask these questions on their own time? I felt so uncomfortable and wished I could do something. Only a minute or so passed before a very loud, assertive voice of a woman halted the parade of white tears. I couldn't see her, she was standing somewhere in the back of the room, and I didn't want to crane my neck.

> "The white people in the room need to be a little more aware of the space we're taking up with all of our questions and all of our misgivings, ok?"

And with that – this loud white woman telling all the new, post-election white people how to act in the space – everyone clapped. I realized in that moment that I could do what she did, if I ever needed to again.

The energy in the room diffused a bit after that. Together, she and Drake had regulated the room and re-centered us. I locked eyes with the kid in the hoodie. His arms were still crossed, but he was finally sitting down. I wondered if he would come back. I thought back to what it felt like that day when I knocked on the door. It's tough being new, and it requires a lot of humility, a lot of listening, and taking a seat when you may have thought you needed to stand up. Still, all the new folks' presence affected the tone of the meeting. I remember one organizer wondering aloud about people in the room who might be there to record and report their activities to the police. This made me nervous, and I was glad I wasn't taking notes that night. Recording anything, creating a paper trail, is often seen as suspect. I knew I wasn't reporting anything to anyone, but sometimes texts take on new audiences in the academy. I didn't feel like I was representing the academy that night, or any night, but I also knew I couldn't just take that identity off and leave it at the door... I was eager to get back to work on the police accountability and public safety campaign.

December 2016

Angela was leading the meeting at TCO that day. She told us we were going to design a new city—fashion it out of thin air. She was using one of those big sheets of paper, the ones with wicked strong adhesive. She started to draw the trunk of a tree using a brown marker. She drew some squiggles at the bottom of the page that looked like little veins. These, she said, were the roots of our city. The roots, the grounding, the foundation of any city, made up of the morals, ethics, and values. She invited us to give breath to some of the roots, and folks began to call out. Some were phrases, some were concepts, some were feelings … *equity, justice, empathy, respect* … The trunk, Angela said, represented the look of the overall system of the city … *communication, safety to worship, good public transit* … A woman who called out *department of peace* contrasted it against a *department of justice*. The whole room seemed to nod in agreement with the thought. Angela said the branches, the next expression of the tree, are the everyday tangible wins … *community first-responders, mandated town-halls, rent stabilization, parental leave* … Angela told us that the leaves on our tree are the manifestations of the aforementioned wins … *fewer prisoners, happy children, street parties, community art, less cars* … Angela created the image by hand. When someone called out "less fear, more eye contact" she drew an eyeball with eyelashes, with an upward arrow, and wrote the words "see me!" next to it (see Figure 3). What took shape is really beautiful.

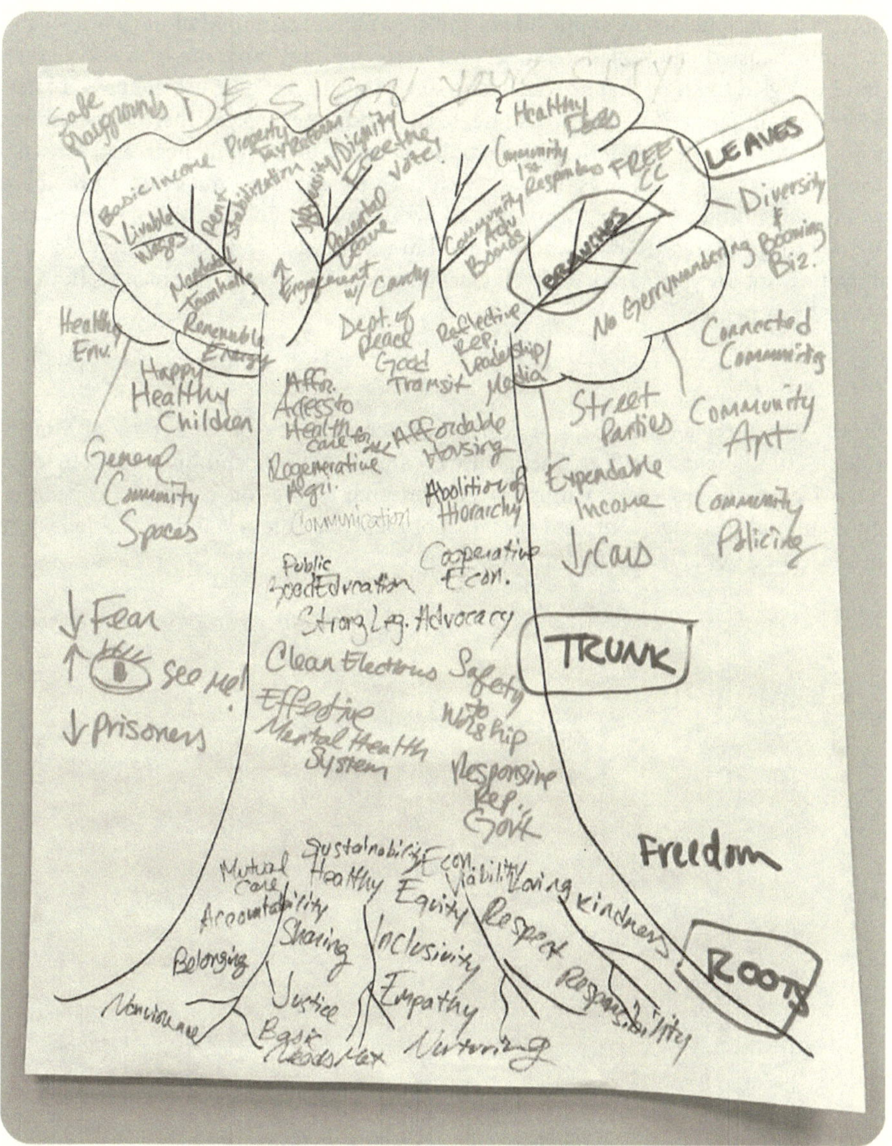

Figure 3. Photo of "Design Your City" activity. The figure shows a large hand-drawn tree on a white sheet of paper with "Design Your City" written across the top. Words emerging from a collective brainstorm are categorized into the tree's roots, trunk, branches, and leaves.

I got the email from Remy while I was commenting on student papers. I wasn't able to go to the city council meeting on account of that stack of papers, and I still wasn't done. But I heard that the council chambers felt similar to how I did when I read about the city council's final budget: $500,000 in one-time funds to invest in community-directed alternative safety strategies in two neighborhoods, one on the north side and one on the south side of the city. YES! I was proud of the work we put in and exhausted emotionally. Remy considered the pilot programs a major victory, and I was glad to know that he was taking some time to rest over the holidays. I knew I'd be back in January, and so would he, to talk about next steps. There was so much work to do, and the discomfort and ambivalence about my whiteness, and how my whiteness was perceived, was, I now saw, just an excuse to get out of doing the hard work. Doing difficult internal work that allows us to show up was the only way to create real social change. Remy's words echoed in my mind as I watched it snow, "I can't do your work for you, Sarah, and you can't do mine. We all have our own work to do. Go get your people."

Author Bio

Sarah Puett received her doctoral degree in Rhetoric from the University of Minnesota in 2018. She currently teaches writing, communication, and diversity courses at Regis University in Denver, Colorado. Her research focuses on composition pedagogy, community engagement, and rhetorics of race. She enjoys stand-up comedy, jazz music, eating out of bowls, and meeting dogs.

Gratitude

Tracey Bullington

Reflection

This short graphic essay portrays an ongoing, personal writing practice: on most days, I receive an email from my friend Victor with a list of things that he feels grateful for, and I respond with a list of my own. I chose a visual genre for this story because I like to picture Victor when I read his emails, imagining where he might have been while writing to me. Drawing brings these imagined scenes to life and connects Victor and I—while we don't often share physical space, our drawn selves are side-by-side on these pages. I began the comic by listing in a notebook the images that came to mind on the topic of gratitude writing. I then wrote a narrative version of the story, circling the phrases that I planned to translate into images. The final comic was drawn and written by hand using pencil, black ink, and watercolor. My process is adapted from instructions in *Making Comics* by Lynda Barry, a book I enthusiastically recommend to others interested in the genre.

I chose to tell the story of this particular literacy practice because my two-person writing community sustains me in ways that I did not initially expect. Our correspondence is a place to celebrate the tiny delights that are generally too small to mention to anyone else, pleasures that might otherwise be overshadowed by struggle, heartbreak, and injustice. Victor and I share an unspoken understanding that while our lists of gratitudes are not a complete recounting of our respective lives, they are a little slice that matters. Through this practice, I have learned to value a type of personal writing that I previously considered unnecessary and even self-indulgent. These emails are one of the ways that I care for myself and for my friend so that I can continue my work as a teacher, researcher, and artist.

GRATITUDE

VICTOR, I CAN STILL REMEMBER THE DAY A FEW WINTERS AGO WHEN YOU ASKED ME TO BE YOUR GRATITUDES BUDDY. YOU SUGGESTED EXCHANGING EMAILS DESCRIBING WHAT WE FELT GRATEFUL FOR EACH DAY.

THANK GOD I GAVE UP TRYING TO WRITE SOMETHING INTERESTING, OR WORSE – PROFOUND...
I'M GRATEFUL FOR CHAI TEA – OR I'M GRATEFUL FOR MY TASTE BUDS AS I DRINK CHAI TEA?

MY GRATITUDES AREN'T SECRETS, BUT LOTS OF TIMES I WRITE THINGS THAT I HAVEN'T TOLD ANYONE ELSE.
AW! BEN & JERRY'S ON SALE AT TRACEY'S SUPERMARKET

SOMETIMES I DON'T WRITE,
AND THE TINY DELIGHTS OF MY DAY GO UNNOTICED
UGH

"HEY, HOPE YOU'RE DOING ALRIGHT, BIG HUGS"

EVEN WITHOUT OUR RITUAL, YOU WOULD HAVE TOLD ME ABOUT THE WEDDING IN LA, THE JOB OFFER, AND THE NEW APARTMENT,

BUT I MIGHT HAVE MISSED HEARING THAT YOU FIXED A FLAT TIRE, SAW A CUTE GUY AT THE GYM, OR TOOK A WEEK OFF OF WRITING.

AND I WOULD NEVER HAVE KNOWN ABOUT THE LIGHT AT YOUR FAVORITE LIBRARY,
OR THE TEMPERATURE OF YOUR THERAPIST'S OFFICE.

WHEN I OPEN YOUR EMAILS, I IMAGINE HOW YOU LOOKED TYPING IT ALL OUT ON YOUR MACBOOK WITH THE WORN OUT KEYBOARD, SITTING AT YOUR KITCHEN TABLE BESIDE A BOWL OF HALF-EATEN OATMEAL.

THERE'S HAIR ON YOUR NECK FROM THE HAIRCUT YOU GAVE YOURSELF.

YOUR WORDS MAKE ME FEEL CLOSE TO YOU. ISN'T THAT MAGIC?
I HOPE VICTOR'S DAY IS GOING OKAY
CAN'T WAIT TO HEAR ABOUT IT

YOU KNEW JUST WHAT I NEEDED.

Author Bio

Tracey Bullington is an artist, teacher, and scholar from New Orleans, Louisiana. She is currently a PhD student at the University of Wisconsin—Madison in the department of Curriculum and Instruction where she studies the role of artmaking in the lives of young people. Tracey has taught comics classes to a variety of learners including multilingual teenagers and professional scientists. More of her creative work can be found on her website: https://www.traceybullington.com/

"Pros & Cons Panel Presentation 2023, Call for Presenters"

Evan Harris

Reflection

"Pros & Cons Panel Presentation 2023, Call for Presenters" came about as I was creating a pros & cons list around resigning from my beloved position as a children's librarian, which I had held for nine years in a small community library close to my home. As I wrote my pros & cons list, I became attuned to the mechanics of making the list, and aware of how making the list was framing my decision making process. The "topics may include but are not limited to" section on the Call represents the progression of ideas I entertained as I created my list, both in concrete terms and more conceptual ones. Meanwhile, I started to think about other people who are also making decisions about their lives and started to imagine their pros & cons lists–how they might approach the lists, how they might think about the list making itself: helpful? reductive? fun? painful? a practical writing exercise–a creative one? And what else?

The Call for Presenters evokes an academic call in order to sneak a sense of legitimacy. Our decision making processes are important and worthy. Yet the Call simultaneously confesses and asserts, with handwriting, and steno paper, and invisibleness, that the game of dress-up is in vain. It reaches outward from the hopelessly and proudly personal and unquantifiable. We are and must be our own legitimators.

I wrote the Call to create a context for a community of pros & cons list makers. It's true that this community may be dismissed as invisible and imaginary, or regarded as simply too impossibly far flung to marshal or define. After all, we don't have a common background or education, we don't have proximity or ideology binding us, we aren't all of the same demographic any way you slice it and we're not even making lists about the same things! We are a conceptual community. Yet pros & cons list makers may still coalesce. Given a point of access (the Call) and an activator (participation through writing), the sense of agency cherished by the pros & cons list maker may be housed and held for those who care to contribute.

There is no deadline, and I am happy imagining the cumulative response honoring pros & cons list makers for their engagement in the process as life goes on.

A Note on the Invitations to Invisible Gatherings Project:

Invitations to Invisible Gatherings is a hybrid genre project that offers invitations to invisible, imaginary, non-physical gatherings of different kinds. The invitations can manifest online through email, social media, and posted or published PDFs as well as outside the ether through the USPS, community bulletin boards, hand to hand exchange, and other distribution. Invitations to Invisible Gatherings proposes an extended sentience around shared experience that is neither virtual nor actual, but imagined. You are cordially invited; your response is sought. The project explores the possibility of unconditional inclusion amongst found participants. The gathering is invisible, but you are not.

Invitations to Invisible Gatherings seeks presentations on classic and contemporary issues in pros & cons list making. The Pros & Cons Panel Presentation is an invisible and imaginary meeting for pros & cons list makers. List makers include me & you and people other than me & you also asking themselves: What in this case is best to do? Presentations may elucidate the theory, practice, or pursuit of a pros & cons list in the tender complex sphere of What Next.

Topics may include but are not limited to:

- Pros & cons lists over the lifespan
- Pros & cons of pros & cons listmaking; the 3rd column; meta concerns
- Issues in parallel construction
- X factors; the unquantifiable; other unknowns
- The frivolous; the shallow; the overly sensitive; tiny details only you care about
- Big picture!
- Entries occuring on both sides of the list; other instances of ambivalence
- My list; your list; other case studies

- All presentations will take place in my thoughts, in your thoughts, and in the thoughts of others
- Submission deadline: you decide
- Pros & cons list makes are invited to submit a presentation by following this QR code:

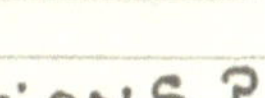

Please contact:
invitationtoinvisiblegathering@gmail.com

Author Bio

Evan Harris is the author of *The Quit* (Fireside, 1996). Her short fiction has appeared in *The Iowa Review*, *Fence*, *Brooklyn Rail*, and *Fairy Tale Review* among other magazines. Evan is a periodic book reviewer for *The East Hampton Star* and is a semi-retired children's librarian, working independently in this beloved field.

A Meta-Staging of the Initial Investigative Operatics Working Group, With [x number of] Original Cast Members Playing All the Parts

Bethany Ides, Fan Wu, Ora Ferdman, and Zoe Tuck

Reflection

In late 2020, Bethany Ides sent an open invitation to prospective collaborators (friends, colleagues, mentors, former students, acquaintances, plus all of their friends, etc.) to meet for eight consecutive weeks on Zoom to explore the contours of a mysterious field called "investigative operatics."[1] A cluster of entangled questions immediately emerged: *What is this phenomenon called "investigative operatics?" How do we study an idea that's still fuzzy, that no one is an expert in yet? How do we go about this study cooperatively and mutually supportively while still getting to know each other?*

"Opera" is the plural of opus. It is a way of conceiving of works or doings as a whole, but perhaps especially as something sprawling and ambitious because all those works and doings must cohere. What holds these works and doings together? A common impetus? A feeling of interdependence? In the roots of the word "investigate" are tracks, traces, *vestiges*.

We consider this piece a flurry of breadcrumbs. It's an axiology, a performance score, a reenactment, a remix, an activity book, a reference list, an archive, and probably other things we haven't figured out yet. It is a text both of and for community writing. Our play insists that the reader play, too. Maybe assign dance moves to the Annotational Schema and wear costumes, for instance. Maybe rotate who plays who. Experiment with sound and lighting, fast and slow, high and low. Some parts may feel like poetry whereas others might feel more like a sing-along. Go with those feelings, see where they lead. Along the way, we've noticed that nonknowledge and incomprehension can often leave space for pleasure.

1. Participants of the Investigative Operatic Working Group included: Linda Austin, Abril Barajas, Alexis Bhagat, Ali Bonfils, Ell Davis, Abner Delina, Bill Dietz, Kerry Downey, Emma BB Doyle, Ora Ferdman, Marshall Gardner, Karen Yvonne Hall, Bethany Ides, Rindon Johnson, Jimie Lerman, Stephanie Loveless, Dakotah Weeks Murphree, Annabel Paran, Michael Quintanilla, Mahshid Rafiei, Julia Santoli, Yasmeen Siddiqui, Toleen Touq, Tim Simonds, Zoe Tuck, Fan Wu, Alex Zandi.

A Note to the Readers

If you are reading this having endured the strict discipline of a conventional PhD program that systematically discourages pleasure and wonder in learning, our hearts go out to you. To meet "academic standards," you likely had to subject yourself to some of the methods of control that academia adopted from colonialism, white supremacy, capitalism, patriarchy, ableism and all the rest. These systems thrive by classifying people, power and intelligence into categories that can be measured, managed and ultimately exploited. To succeed in academia, a person must accept and abide by rules defining what's worth studying and why, and how (not to mention when and where). The process can be filled with drudgery. And then, the folks who struggle through that sometimes become gatekeepers themselves and end up perpetuating the whole thing (as much as they probably also hate it), worried for their jobs or feeling stuck in a system they're now complicit in. The rotten truth is that, within institutional systems like academia that are alienating by design, almost everybody is being used, and even brave innovations must be retrofitted to suit that structure of authority in order to function.

If you are reading this, feeling like you don't fit in academia—if you dropped out of school, found an unbeaten path, and/or created your own hacks and workarounds to immerse yourself in the ideas you're interested in among people with whom there's reciprocity and shared respect—we are with you. (That's us, too.) If you want to hold up the elders who are not (yet) embraced by the academic canon by exploring strategies for study and mutual support that are meaningful to you but which the gatekeepers may have deemed too "inaccessible" or difficult, this is for you. We trust that you can handle strangeness.

So-called "experimental literature" is an experiment simply because nobody knows yet what will happen, what it will do, what it's capable of. Experimentation is a process of working (and playing) with pure potential. We experiment because the experimenters before us taught us what else was out there beyond the accepted standards. They taught us to love feeling ourselves on the edge of what's becoming possible. When we experiment, we are actively developing practices for becoming free.

Here's our play.

A Meta-Staging of the Initial Investigative Operatics Working Group, With [x number of] Original Cast Members Playing All the Parts

An empty theater. A busy internet.

After rehashing for weeks what, in fact, did or might have happened; after scavenging scaffolding remnants, attempting to retroactively configure a plan then comparing that plan to the original intent; after wondering: did our meetings become sequential when they were only meant to be serial? How variable is research as a practice or process; as investigative; as pluripotent? At what point does the expectation of what something might become dissolve into what it is?

Annotational Schema:

⇝ PAVANE (moving through)
⧳ WIRETAPPING (listening in)
⇉ STAKEOUT (watching out)
⏀ ARIA (holding on)

Figure: Trace the perimeter of the visual space of your screen—the limits of your image of yourself ⇝. Dim your screen till it's dark and you can no longer see others.[2]

Counter Figure: Grammatically sliding into a place as a matter of occurrence, of becoming referrable. ⇉ The phantom "what" that we are studying "here" lingers endophorically, from within (the common text of a continuing

2. Directions provided during Annabel Paran's workshop on/of/from Ralph Lemon's practice and processes, co-facilitated with Marshall Gardner for the Investigative Operatics Working Group, February 7, 2021.

discourse). It's always there in the periphery but, like an aged star, seems to disappear if you try and look straight at it.

Chorus: The common text glimmers, too.

Countra Dancer: The common text is the discourse in its continuing as it's continuing, comprised both of evident and imagined transcripts, equally referable, whether via digital or non-digital memory files. One is better suited to conceiving of exactitude and information that is extrinsic to change, whereas the other is sensitive, affected by whimsy and decay.

Flashback.[3]

Like anything becomes knowable as itself, we need a name, we need a thing to say and say we're all gathered around. An organizational arrangement of letters and ideas about order that is familiar and pronounceable enough. A real symbolic point of egress between here and there. ⏀ Or between major reading and minor reading; the difference between concepts that feel already ordered by other importances and concepts that change direction on a dime. And the interstice; a crease that runs between them where the sweat gathers a scent. We'll tell by smell. In French, *sillage* is the quality of integrity a scent sustains after its discharging agent has passed—how well I sense you later and for how long ⧫. Which is a way of qualifying value by way of dissipative currents. ⇉ Sniffing and tracking Investigative Operatics while also emitting an olfactory trail. So many fugitive particles intermingling uncontrollably assures us that we are sensing both ourselves and others in that alembic "what."

⏀ **Proxy Agent:** It's hard, though. It's hard to—what happens when you—when you arrive at a doorway, intending to claim access to a doorway. And you encounter another hallway. Does this path correspond with a motivated tract or does it trace a meandering course of always already

3. In Yve-Alain Bois's Introduction to Lygia Clark's "Nostalgia of the Body," we find his recollection of Clark demonstrating a flashback sequence in real time for an audience of one (Bois); opening boxes, "unpacking the oldest things first.[...].Nothing that came out of them was made simply to be seen and not touched."

annexed vexation?

Interpreter: I hear you saying that arriving "here," wherever or whenever one does, always means beginning, and beginning always means a backlog of processing information/sensation. Does that sound right to you?

No reply.

Interpreter: Arriving "here" by signal?

Proxy Agent: All I could think of was the world of sports; the world of gestures, maneuvers, playbook diagrams, allegiances, starting positions. I couldn't remember how I got here/"here." Did I arrive like a scientist? Like a detective? ⇜ Or, like a drunken lover stumbling through the snow, my footsteps fading into ellipses ⇜?

No reply.

Proxy Agent: All I could remember was an old television commercial panning down a limitless passageway lined with endless doors and windows. The jingle repeated the same phrase forward then backward, that's how lost we were.

Interpreter: Grammatic function and dysfunction seeming indistinguishable what's implicit and not yet. Every small and large pronoun already mid-doing. Does that sound…? ⏀

***Intra-* between; *mural* the walls.**

The chorus of clairvoyants sing from behind a screen or curtain ❣, tuning to remote areas of interest.

Tuning to Tina Campt: We can engage a listening sense when encountering images/documents, engaging their anteriority decidedly haptically, ⇉ requiring interrogation of our encounter both at the gateway entry level of opening an archive as well as with the content inside. "It is a method that reckons with the fissures, gaps, and interstices emerge when we refuse to accept the 'truth' of images and archives," particularly those that institutions use to regulate and reproduce subjecthood through. We can disorder, disrupt that.[4]

Myung Mi Kim: A poem (like an image or a document, recording, or live event) might become conceivable "through cycles of erosion and accretion."

To encounter and to problematize the political and economical terms that function to determine and codify legibility. [...]And in that process, inside the procedures of work and of work proceeding, note: node and pressure point, song making and song gesture. Track: descant, sedimentations, tributaries in any several directions ↭. Show stress, show beat, show changes and alterations in pitch and accentuals. Syllables or tempo stored, ruptured, emended. A valence of first and further tongues. A fluctuating topography, a ringing of verve or nerve–transpiring[5]

Pause/Interval: ⇉ We look for evidence of Investigative Operatics in moments of exchange, interchange. We think of anecdotes and scraps as often as titles of pieces or names of artists. We try

4. Any book might be said to stage an encounter But to touch the pages of this book and to observe oneself doing so is an investigative operatic act.

5. Kim seems to be addressing and revamping Ed Dorn's project of Investigative Poetics. Kim here invites "tending to the speculative" as part of that project, as an active readerly (as much as writerly), intratemporal process.

out methods or habits as means of finding loose bits, what might come unstuck from applications of quantifiable value.

Tuning to Isabelle Stengers: We think of interstices that create their own dimensions and, extensively, each their own scope in terms of what and whom they concern, that open intervals for what might be becoming knowable. "Effectively, the interstice doesn't give any response, but it generates new questions" (Stengers).[6]

Sample Question: Can we return the "folk" to "art?"

Tuning, in Gestures: Ishmael Reed recounts how Simon Ortiz met with angry frustration the suggestion of a single location or particular method of education or institutional style being deemed primary with regard to human creative effort/ spirit. Ortiz insisted, "I would guide any Native American away from the idea that one place is the center of American poetry today," referring to Naropa and to an attitude about culture "belong[ing] to the people" that he was taught in the Acoma village he grew up in" (Reed). "Handiwork and more: belief and art: ingenuity and concept, paying careful attention to things," Ortiz wrote later, describing a communal building process and how he came to know from his own involvement in that process that the house would "last a long time" because of all of these qualities, but especially humility (Ortiz).

Tuning to Gertrude Stein: "Act so that there is no use in a center"). A refusal, also an initiative.

Email Impersonator: Let's consider these terms together as interrelated biomass: "experimental

6. Stengers's *Capitalist Sorcery: Breaking the Spell* is a book that is curiously too expensive for most interested readers to own in hard copy (what few copies seem to exist), however it is widely available in PDF online. Its verisimilar publication is so prevalent that the book seems almost hypothetical.

research" and "visitation," along with peopled pronouns and a pyre of commodified/monetized applications of these processes out from which a ladder boldly extends. Shoots and ladders. Buckets of phosphorescent oceanic bits of life and death. The matter can be re-stirred to re-light it up again, again; re- re-.

Enthusiastic Participant: Let's co-, co-; as supple, as more porous than more dogmatic and hierarchical formations (academia, nonprofit world, certain political or activist milieus). And being thrown, like a piece of stellar matter, outward, but in a patterned and collocated way. A spiral arm, extending and (de)forming as it/we extend/s. And mapping more in the sense of interested traversal rather than as extractive aide-mémoire. Let's be concerned with slippage, the transverse archipelogic of an isolarion (becoming scattered?). Plural AND coordinated. To be "here" you have to be coordinated to execute an intention within the social body or, by extension, to explore the possibilities for social action. Or to use the (nonce) word *aesthetion*, as analogue (or adjutant) for action. And something even softer, somatic, preverbal like circulatory systems ♦.

(Having the will, but also the wish.)

Sample Question: How would this sound as community in the active voice?

An Open Chord: Like scouting, contour, reverberation; like "unnamed sensibilities" (Amacher), "a feature-length we-don't-know" and an "undertak[ing] to improvise something better than that which has been written" (Greaves,);[7] like smaragdinatic tabulation, spooky action; like reading billets.

William Greaves: "It doesn't matter whether or

7. As a strategy for emergent organizing, *Symbiopsychotaxiplasm, Take One* became the bookends for the particular series of "episodes" this particular libretto or digital architecture or textual encounter concerns.

not you understand it. The important thing is that we surface from this production experience with something that is entirely exciting and creative as a result of our collective efforts."[8]

Fred Rogers: "What's important is you can pretend about things and dream about things that you don't completely understand."[9]

Cameron Awkward-Rich: Trying to "interrogate the assumption that this kind of elegiac memorialization—keeping the dead alive, with us—is actually an ethical thing to be doing, if what that means is keeping them alive in a world that did little to support their living."

And not knowing and not-knowing meaning needing to. And desiring to know how to.

A plea, an apology, a eulogy, a rejection.[10]

Make a selection, then extract a reasonably irreducible part of the selection.

This is a _____ for people who want to ____ about how performed and prospective doings _________ our senses of/for _______ ____________, that is: _____-________

8. Greaves, playing the part of himself/Director addressing the cast and crew (playing the parts of themselves) during the filming of what would amount to *Symbiopsychotaxiplasm, Take One*.

9. This statement delivered directly to the camera during an episode about opera-making in the Land of Make-Believe, appears in Rogers' handwritten notes in his archives as "You can pretend @ things you don't completely understand and dream about." This document can be found at the Fred Rogers Center at Saint Vincent College in Rogers's hometown of Latrobe, PA.

10. This guideline was given by Abril Barajas and Michael Quintanilla, co-facilitators of an experimental engagement with the tactics of both Lygia Clark and Linda Mary Montano for the Investigative Operatics Working Group, January 10, 2021. Very memorably, each set of ameliorative directions were then enacted or recited by a different group, (intensely) demonstratively.

on purpose, and how that predicate in turn becomes __________. So, in practical, __________ terms, we're talking about: _______, _______, _____, __________, _________, _______, _______, barn raisings, ________, ________, _______ ____, __________, ______, etc. For the sake of discussion, we'll call these "convocational technologies" to help us better determine how manners and language pattern our habits of participancy.

Each week, volunteer members of the working group (such as yourself) will co-facilitate explorations of work by practitioners[11] whose projects pose contemplative contours for investigative operatics. Volunteer facilitators are welcome to invent and deviate however they choose so long as the _-____ ____ ______ __ ___________ ______. _ _____ are intentionally left open for additions to the repertoire.

There might be

a. problem solving;
b. maybe dramatic reenacting;
c. riffing;
d. maybe explicating every question ↭;
e. every implication or ramification related;
f. maybe translating;
g. transposing;
h. or transitioning a premise from one context to another;
i. maybe dissolving future pasts;

A Para-cultural Communicant, a Litany[12]

⏀ Entering increased dimensions, endless hallways, limitless expectancy.
The echo down the corridor manifests as distinct from the echo chamber.

11. Practitioners whose oeuvres and preoccupations were conscientiously contemplated and possibly reappropriated as informing a provisional understanding of investigative operatics during the course of the Investigative Operatics Working Group meetings included: William Greaves, Fred Rogers, Augusto Boal, Maryanne Amacher, José Maceda, Lygia Clark, Linda Mary Montano, Dylan Robinson, Juan Downey, Ursula K. LeGuin, Anna and Lawrence Halprin, CAConrad, Yukio Waguri and Tatsumi Hijikata, and Ralph Lemon (in that order).

12. This is a riff on a phrase Juan Downey uses to describe his "utopian reformulation of the road trip," which was jotted down during a discussion of Downey's "Fake Anthropology" co-facilitated by Alexis Bhagat and Stephanie Loveless for the Investigative Operatics Working Group, January 17, 2021.

When these meetings have ceased, we'll have asked ourselves and each other: how did I get here?[13]
The awkwardness of a process corresponds to the frostiness of the route less travelled.

Meaning: did this path correspond with a tract or does it trace a meandering course of vexation?
From trace to tract.

Arriving just in time to deal with the problems of processing a bulk of information.
And just in time to valorize the counter-processes of nonknowledge.

⇉ Just because you can observe a distance as awful long doesn't mean it's in your mind.
Foreshortened, as of space in the role of the bully of time.

What happens to displacement, what looks so much like coincidence (transience?).
Probably the way affinity is like weather, how your body can tell what's happening by the measures of change.

Instinctively, your and my "I"s all arriving, not feeling nauseous, not listening hungrily ♦♦♦, but needing an ethics.
What could be more exhausting. What could be more emotional.

This history of holding extended, sometimes contentious, discussion intersects with the history of considering fairness in financial transactions.
Can you say more about that?

When it is alright to walk away, to extricate oneself from the situation, to consider one's effort no longer applicable to the matter at hand, to become free to pursue significance elsewhere; to find closure.
When operatics is taken as the subject of investigation, I found there to be no closure, but the eternal momentum of investigation: investigation's pure energy.

How a person becomes governable and how a situation becomes governable are both matters of propriety, of conceiving of an interrelated—if not intractable—bundle of rights.
We all know how a room smells when no one knows who holds the power.

Another way of describing rights is as predictions.
A swarm of normies is the oracle of their own entitlement.

Not only do I have rights to this now, but in the future also—maybe because I bought

13. This question, posed to participants during Bhagat's and Loveless's workshop, echoes familiarly in a dream, a song, a long stare into the void.

it, because it was bestowed to me, or because I've always considered this intrinsically mine.
Colonialism as a means to scribble your own prices on the commodities' tags.

A financial transaction need conclude so that a performance of ownership might commence ↭↭↭.
Nothing falls into my possession; I can't act in belief as though I own anything; I can't close the deal on this feeling.

If there were no agreed upon amount that one is owed or indebted, then there is property.
Do you want to buy psilocybin therapy stocks with me, on the speculative market?

The particular price's symbolic value is always meant to be commensurate with the amount of pain, discomfort, or disappointment involved in concluding matters.
What's the symbolic value of investigative operatics if there was no pain, multiple flights of glee, a bit of boredom, little sea-flares of curiosity—how to symbolize this bundle?

Expectation to constantly own, to maintain ownership and ward off expropriation—what could be more exhausting. What could be more emotional.
Not feeling nauseous, not listening hungrily, needing an ethics. Φ

Coda.

After rehashing for weeks what mimeses, commentaries, heuristics or puzzle games, what communal responses to or participation in senses of the coming-something were maybe activated or represented, in collapsing valences, relaxing overlaps, we (the self-appointed Chorus) are still wondering, as if on repeat:

How the figure/counter-figure's untitled individual
historicality is acting out again, rearranging itself, replacing its
recordings with its incarnations, its identifications
with its openings. These dear conveners & their
['where,'] with all its official documents covered over, that could draw
itself around the name

of non-recognition // contingency of
knowledge. They are suspicious of becoming situated
too easily. They host combinatory events and
invite plural modes of participation. Amateurs

in spacesuits *evince* a sideways entrance[:]
unlimited doors linking ‘convocational
technologies’—potlucks, parades, tours,
workshops, protests, barn raisings, communal camping, research labs, ceremonies,
dances—

there at the precipice of *evoke[,]* but no piggy toes curl by evocation alone.
The finger(toe) score
brings the body into it, carries language out and
over the edge. Only a pinky
each to steer the ship of fools to markets, homes, meats, nothingness,
barn doors, crying for weeks on end,
to swiftly drift past vaster reaches.

It springs to mind, this whichever-togetherness,
its spoonfuls of stories, of standards, of didacticism offset by
dramamine high gone threshingmachinelike; the pursuit of an elocution
all the more masterful for sputtering out too soon, or too
slow, too sly to appoint one or another to rescue
the entire lyrical community approaches.

⏀ ***Congregation for Little Miss Muffet who twirls kidsticks, sups on truffle soup.***
(Stomp feet, spit, act like a spider, whisper “truffle soup” in each other’s ears slowly ⊠, write as a recipe.)

Convocation for the choirs who traverse the fission territories feet on coal.
(Spread toes, spread fingers, scratch each other’s backs, tickle each other’s feet, write up a contract ↭.)

Constituent pluripotent energies: sulfur tongues & a geometry of comfort.
(Blow a kiss to someone in the room, curse someone in the room, build a platform for that.)

Constellation of crushes and distrust, that old sluicing crossroads.
⇉ (Make eye contact with someone, break it, repeat, design an interchange.)

Opera **ultimately open-throated i.e. a Yes across the silliness.**
(Sound out “yes” repeatedly, differently each time, come up with different words for yes, sound them out simultaneously/overlapping in no order.)

Investigation **as though the magnifying glass were made of lava, half-runners down the “tear here” line of Pandora’s Box.**
(Improvise a dialogue void of meaning, transcribe it, perform again using

the transcription but swap lines.)

I rest my case, i.e. *now I awake.*
(Applause.) ⦶

(June 2021)

References

Awkward-Rich, Cameron. "The Rumpus Poetry Book Club Chat with Cameron Awkward-Rich." *The Rumpus*. December 24, 2019. *www.therumpus.net.*

Amacher, Maryanne. *Selected Writings and Interviews*, edited by Amy Cimini and Bill Dietz, New York: Blank Forms, 2020.

Campt, Tina. *Listening to Images.* Duke UP, 2017.

Clark, Lygia and Yve-Alain Bois. "Nostalgia of the Body." *October* 69 (Summer), 1994, pp. 85-109. JSTOR. https://doi.org/10.2307/778990

González, Julieta. "Notes on Juan Downey's Project for a Fake Anthropology," in *Juan Downey: El Ojo Pensante*. Santiago: Fundación Telefónica, 2011. 201-12.

Kim, Myung Mi. "Anacrusis." *How2* 1, no. 2, 1999..

Mister Rogers' Neighborhood. Episode 1565. "A Star for Kitty." 28:31, May 9, 1986. www.misterrogers.org/episodes/a-star-for-kitty-opera/.

Ortiz, Simon J.. *After and Before the Lightning.* Tucson: The U of Arizona P, 1994.

Reed, Ishmael. "American Poetry: A Buddhist Take-over?" *Black American Literature Forum* 12, no. 1 (Spring), 1978.

Spicer, Jack, and Peter Gizzi. *The House That Jack Built : The Collected Lectures of Jack Spicer*. Middletown: Wesleyan UP, 1998.

Stein, Gertrude. *Tender Buttons*. Mineola: Dover Publications, 1997.

Stengers, Isabelle. *Capitalist Sorcery: Breaking the Spell.* London: Palgrave Macmillan, 2011.

Symbiopsychotaxiplasm, Take One. DVD, Directed by William Greaves. 1968. The Criterion Collection, 2005.

Author Bios

Bethany Ides teaches Humanities & Media Studies at Pratt Institute where she is Adjunct Professor with Certificate of Continuous Employment. A writer, researcher and community organizer, she pursues all forms of speculative folklife: evented being-togetherness that intrepidly eludes commodification, monetization and standardization. Her recent work appears or is forthcoming in *Radical Teacher Journal*, *Shifter*, Ear|Wave|Event, the *Candidate Journal: Psychoanalytic Currents*, and in the book *Tongue & Cheek* (Montez Press).

Fan Wu is a poet, performer, pedagogue, and puppet of crushes. He's currently working on a project that entwines Zhuangzi and Bataille in the territories of the Formless, the Useless, and the Unknowable. You can read his work online at *C Magazine*, *Capilano Review*, and *In the Mood Magazine*.

Ora Ferdman is owner/operator of Fora Construction, a trans-centric design & build firm based in the Rondout Valley region of New York. She is also an artist whose work has been supported by residencies and fellowships from Habitable Spaces (TX), Art Camp (ME), SenseLab (QC) and the Good Works Institute (NY).

Zoe Tuck was born in Texas, became a person in California, and now lives in Massachusetts. She is the author of *Bedroom Vowel* (Bunny Presse), *Terror Matrix* (Timeless, Infinite Light) and the chapbooks *Vape Cloud of Unknowing* (Belladonna*) and The *Book of Bella* (DoubleCross Press). In addition to teaching private creative writing and literature classes, Zoe is the co-host of The *But Also* reading series, the co-editor of *Hot Pink Magazine*, and is an active member of the Belladonna* Collaborative.

Against Forgetting: Quilt Pieces and Reflection

Susan Naomi Bernstein

Reflection

My partner and I moved back to Queens, NewYork, from Arizona in 2018, and we were pleased to discover our neighborhood Center for Older Adults. Our small workshop group of older adults, which NYC defines as anyone over 60, met in a small room in the basement of the Center and shared poems of poets we admired (Audre Lorde; Joy Harjo; Pablo Neruda; links via URL below) and then wrote poems together.

The next year brought the catastrophe of the Coronavirus pandemic. Our city suffered disasters, emergencies, and lockdowns, and our local community suffered loss upon loss. We were reminded that, as older adults, we were among the populations most vulnerable to dying from the coronavirus. The Center closed for in-person congregate activities and shifted to survival mode focusing on food distribution for those of us who were home-bound for the foreseeable future.

By late Spring of 2020, the Center was able to set up Zoom activities for our community, including the poetry workshop with my partner and me facilitating. Around this time George Floyd (link via URL below) was murdered by the police in Minneapolis. The workshop was much smaller and all of us were white, so my partner and I decided to focus on the work of Black writers, especially James Baldwin (link via URL below).

Quilting—and the plan for a coronavirus quilting project—came much later. After lockdown, my long-diagnosed generalized anxiety grew much worse. Making art offered a means of articulating swirling emotions that seemed to elude written language. Quilting became a way of free writing without words, an attempt to bring together disparate pieces of what the pandemic had ripped apart.

I had come to quilting several years before in Arizona. Stuck inside for months in relentless heat, I quilted to give a neurodivergent visual and kinesthetic form to my academic work. I had a sewing room and a collection of fabric screen prints from the Occupy Wall Street Screen CoopPrinters (link via URL below). One of the artists suggested I make a quilt with the prints, and became a means against forgetting Occupy Wall Street and those brief extraordinary moments in Zuccotti Park.

But when I moved back to an extremely small living space in NYC I gave up quilting because I didn't seem to have either the room or the long hot summers to do this work. The pandemic changed this.

The coronavirus quilt evolved from mourning my father's death from the coronavirus before vaccines were available, which I write about in the essay "The Body Cannot Sustain an Insurrection" (link via the QR code below), but it had gestated for nearly two years, until my partner and I caught the virus in December 2022.

We were fully vaccinated, and our cases were mild. During quarantine, I embroidered a bird from a cross stitch birthday gift. I spent quarantine embroidering the bird, and wondering how I could make an embroidered coronavirus, a monstrous virus, a virus of many colors with angry mRNA eyes, noses, and mouths. Using a diagram I found on the internet, I made a paper pattern, then traced the pattern on a reusable grocery bag. The corona virus quilt was born.

Even as the national emergency was ending, the pandemic did not. 1.13 + million people were still dead, my father among them. Like Occupy, I did not want the lessons from this time to be forgotten, so I wrote Against Forgetting on the back of an old canvas patch, words I remembered from the poet Carolyn Forche (link via URL below) and embroidered over the letters.

My partner took the poetry workshop from Zoom to an email list that now includes Center staff as well as older adult members. I still write with the group from time to time, half-finished poems lie like fabric swatches meant to try to describe the indescribable pandemic:

> Should I offer words to ease the stress?
> As the flood gathers and the waters press

I cannot think how to connect the words to anything else. Instead, I return to my coronavirus quilt, working toward completion, stitch by neverending stitch.

Against Forgetting: Quilt Pieces and Reflection

Please scan the QR code for access to the material linked above.

Author Bio

Susan Naomi Bernstein (she/they) quilts, writes, and teaches in Queens, NY. She blogs for Bedford Bits, and her recent publications include "The Body Cannot Sustain an Insurrection" in the *Journal of Multimodal Rhetorics* and "After Basic Writing" in *TETYC*. Susan has exhibited her quilts in Phoenix, Arizona and Brooklyn, NY. She thanks S. Cormany and I. James for their peer review insights and support.

www.ingramcontent.com/pod-product-compliance
Lightning Source LLC
LaVergne TN
LVHW051004080826
845145LV00009B/2454

* 9 7 8 1 6 4 3 1 7 4 6 4 8 *